Carle M. Hunt
Kenneth W. Oosting
Robert Stevens

David Loudon
R. Henry Migliore

Strategic Planning
for Private Higher Education

Pre-publication
REVIEWS,
COMMENTARIES,
EVALUATIONS . . .

"**H**unt, Oosting, Stevens, Loudon, and Migliore have done an excellent job of creating a book that helps colleges and universities work their vision through plans to reality. For beginners in strategic planning, there are step-by-step worksheets and instructions. For those further along, there are challenging and informative directions to keep your institution focused and make sure your mission is accomplished.

I wish this book was available when I learned strategic planning for my college. Instead of having to sift through the language of business as I did, the authors allow higher education professionals the opportunity to learn in their own language with helpful higher education illustrations. This volume will make a solid contribution to the college and university community."

Roger B. Edrington, PhD
Executive Vice President,
San Jose Christian College,
San Jose, California

"**I** wish this book had been available when I began my work as a college president 12 years ago. It has an impressive blend of theoretical insights from the best sources on strategic planning coupled with a very practical set of instructions. The authors work out of clear definitions. This work can assist all of those who will be involved in the planning process, especially a strategic planning committee. It is free of jargon and parts of it could be used directly in a retreat for board members or in a workshop for faculty.

The work is timely in noting that we live in an age of unprecedented challenge and opportunity for private higher education. The approach to leadership will be especially helpful to those who need to better understand the tough fiber of campus culture as well as accelerating change in the external environment. Too often in academic life we allow our concerns to be focused on the immediate and on our part of the whole. Strategic planning takes us out five to ten years and directs our attention to the entire college. Persistent leadership is required to think and act strategically.

This book is a time-saver. We have all been in strategic planning committee meetings that consume time and attention without addressing the key questions. All of the significant parts of the planning process come with very helpful worksheets. In some cases there are even assessment guides to encourage high-quality strategic thinking.

Both presidents and boards will benefit from a concise summary of the key financial ratios and percentages that allow a college to compare with peer institutions and with the clear objectives that emerge from the planning process. The authors bring a rich background of actual administration experience and work on dozens of campuses as consultants. They have done excellent work as instructors and mentors and their work deserves sustained attention by administrative, faculty, and board members who want to translate vision into effective higher education."

Victor Stoltzfus, PhD
*Professor of Sociology
and President Emeritus,
Goshen College, Indiana*

More pre-publication
REVIEWS, COMMENTARIES, EVALUATIONS . . .

"The authors have provided a much-needed resource for private higher education, the largest but most frequently overlooked sector in America. This is a manual for the beginner in strategic planning as well as for the experienced planner in any level of education.

Make no mistake, the breadth of perspective does not reduce the content to superficial treatment of the topics. Each well-written chapter is crafted to bring clarity and precision, along with useful definitions. The chapter 'Defining Your Mission and Vision' illustrates proactive thinking with its insights on vision articulation, leadership planning, steps to taking action, and suggested applications.

One of the most useful components is the inclusion of a set of guiding questions at the end of each section. These serve not only as a review, but as a stimulus for provoking action for further analysis, refinement, and desired results. The authors have included case studies, and sample action plans move the reader from the theoretical to the practical level.

Unlike the scores of publications that cross my desk, *Strategic Planning for Private Higher Education* is a book to keep, a book to use."

Sister Marie Roseanne Boneini, PhD
President, Immaculata College,
Immaculata, Pennsylvania

"*Strategic Planning for Private Higher Education* is a complete review of the planning process that benefits both the novice and the experienced planner. Equipped with examples, checklists, and case studies, it is a practical document that encourages action as well as thought. It is well written and easy to read, a user-friendly document that supports readers as they initiate strategic planning at their institutions. The authors share from their vast experience in strategic planning, providing insight into how the process really works so that the reader can accelerate up the learning curve and avoid many of the mistakes that often cause planning programs to stall out or slow down."

David A. Dyson, PhD
Dean, School of Business,
Oral Roberts University

"This is a book that should be found on the desk of every administrator. It is clear, concise, and contains practical checklists that serve as a handy guide in the strategic planning process. The book is uniquely written to provide a blueprint for ongoing checks of an institution's health in

The Haworth Press, Inc.

Strategic Planning
for Private Higher Education

HAWORTH Marketing Resources
Innovations in Practice & Professional Services
William J. Winston, Senior Editor

Strategic Planning for Private Higher Education

Carle M. Hunt
Kenneth W. Oosting
Robert Stevens
David Loudon
R. Henry Migliore

The Haworth Press
New York • London

The Haworth Press, Inc., 10 Alice Street, Binghamton, NY 13904-1580

Cover designed by Donna M. Brooks.

Library of Congress Cataloging-in-Publication Data

Strategic planning for private higher education / Carle M. Hunt . . . [et al.].
    p. cm.
  Includes bibliographical references and index.
  ISBN 0-7890-0191-8 (alk. paper)
    1. Private universities and colleges–United States–Planning. 2. Strategic planning–United States. 3. Education. Higher–Aims and objectives–United States. 4. Private universities and colleges–United States–Administration. I. Hunt, Carle M.
LB2328.52.U6S87 1996
378′.04′0973–dc20
                                          96-40976
                                           CIP

CONTENTS

ABOUT THE AUTHORS

Carle M. Hunt, PhD, is Professor of Management at Regent University, Virginia Beach, Virginia, where he teaches strategic management, leadership, nonprofit organization management, and human resource management at the graduate level both in the School of Business and the School of Education. He was formerly Academic Vice President at Regent University and Chief Business Officer at two other private universities. Dr. Hunt is a consultant to the higher education community in the areas of strategic planning and management.

Kenneth W. Oosting, PhD, is founder and President of Oosting and Associates, Inc., a professional academic and management consulting firm located in Franklin, Tennessee that provides services to colleges, universities, and other organizations in the areas of curriculum development, degree completion, and marketing of programs to adult students. Dr. Oosting has served as Academic Dean of Milligan College in Johnson City, Tennessee and as President of a community college. Recently, he served as the interim Academic Dean for Puget Sound Christian College in Edmonds, Washington. He has been a consultant to over 70 colleges, universities, and seminaries.

Robert Stevens, PhD, is Professor of Marketing at Northeast Louisiana University where he teaches marketing research, marketing management, statistics, strategic management, and principles of marketing. Dr. Stevens is the author of 11 books and more than 100 articles. He has served as a consultant to local, regional, and national firms for research projects, feasibility studies, and market planning, and has been a partner in a marketing research company.

David Loudon, PhD, is Professor of Marketing and Head of the Department of Management and Marketing in the College of Business Administration at Northeast Louisiana University. He is the author of over 50 articles and six books on topics such as consumer behavior, marketing and strategic planning in churches and nonprofit organizations, and legal services marketing. Dr. Loudon has conducted research in the United States, Europe, and Latin America on a variety of topics, including the application of marketing concepts to nontraditional areas. He has served as a consultant and is President of a computer software firm.

R. Henry Migliore, PhD, is Professor of Strategic Planning and Management at Northeastern State University, University Centre at Tulsa where he teaches both graduate and undergraduate courses. He was formerly Dean of the Oral Roberts University School of Business. Dr. Migliore is heavily involved in consulting for national and multinational firms and is the author of numerous articles and books, including *An MBO Approach to Long-Range Planning, Strategic Long-Range Planning,* and *Strategic Planning and Management.*

Preface

The priorities in the preparation of this book have been, first, to create an understanding of the importance of planning within private higher education. This assumes an understanding of these unique institutions, which is the basis for the recommendations in this book. We believe that private higher education needs to be more effective in planning its future in order to have a viable future. The challenges to private higher education today are unprecedented, with a rate of change that is accelerating.

Institutions can go along for the ride—until the ride ends. Or each institution can shape its future within the scope of its vision and mission. We believe that, even though the challenges are the greatest they have been for private higher education, the opportunities are also unprecedented. It is up to the college, university, seminary, graduate school, technical school, or other form of private higher education to determine which path it wishes to take. We urge that the path be one in which the institution takes a proactive avenue toward shaping its own destiny through a program of ongoing, continuous strategic planning.

The importance we address carries over to other forms of private education such as the private academy and preschool as well as elementary and secondary schools. While the principles and illustrations in this book are for private higher education, much of the material can be easily applied to other forms of private education.

The second priority in writing this book has been to provide an understanding of principles as they relate to planning in institutions. What dynamics occur when institutions attempt to create a specific future? What is a vision statement and what role does a mission statement play in guiding an institution? What should be addressed first and then what sequence of events after that is advisable?

Third, we wanted to present material that was theoretically sound but practically oriented. We want the reader to be able to put the concepts presented to immediate use in decision making for the future of an institution. We have included worksheets throughout to help readers develop their own strategic plans. The book is intended for the practitioner in private higher education as well as for the practice-oriented student.

The fourth priority has been to provide a case study to help the reader identify with situations that might carry over to situations faced on the home campus. The intent was to give inspiration to leaders on how to make planning happen in a manner that will change the future. The case of Thorndyke College (presented in the Appendixes) is intended to illustrate a number of points throughout the book. We have built the case to reflect what our experiences tell us is typical of colleges of this type.

A review of the table of contents will suggest that the authors believe that institutions should have a vision that is understood, shared, and acted upon. This vision will lead to an operating mission statement that must guide every decision of the institution. At the same time, planning is always done within an external environment that constantly changes and a culture within the institution that will often favor the status quo or the past rather than an unknown future.

Leadership is essential to planning. Only leadership can affect the campus culture in a manner that will provide the courage for an institution to move into partly charted waters, and to catch the vision and mission of what an institution could be through team effort and shared enthusiasm applied to a strategic planning process.

Planning is an opportunity for leadership. Those who would provide leadership in an institution should become involved in strategic planning for the institution. Through this process, the whole future of the institution is placed in front of those who have the responsibility for the leadership needed to forge the future that is most appropriate for that institution.

We take the position that strategic planning in an institution can transform it, can reengineer it, and can make it into a force that leads other institutions instead of following them. It encourages an institution to become the norm instead of the institution which measures itself by the norms. Strategic planning allows the institution to be a leader rather than a follower or observer of the higher education scene.

While the world around us is changing rapidly, many institutions today will be affected by others in major ways and thus behave in a reactive mode. A few institutions will effectively plan and thus help to create the future by interacting with the changing world. Having that impact, however, requires more than marginally incremental change within an institution, and cannot be accomplished without strategic planning. It requires leadership at all levels within the institution to catch the vision of what the institution can be, to develop a mission statement about what the institution is striving to do right now and in the immediate future, and to see how strategic planning will be utilized to bring that vision and mission about for the benefit of the students the institution has included within its mission.

Acknowledgments

A book is seldom the work of the authors alone but involves the efforts of a great number of people. We would specifically like to thank the following people for their contributions: JoAnna Hunt, who encouraged Carle Hunt to develop the ideas of this book; Jackie Oosting, who helped Ken Oosting to see how he might help others in higher education; Melinda Calhoun, who tirelessly typed the original versions of the manuscript; Melissa Hewlett and Sherry Stewart, graduate students in the MBA program at Northeast Louisiana University, for their research assistance; and the administration of Northeast Louisiana University for their support of this project. Finally, we acknowledge the help of Oosting and Associates copy editors Diana Walker and Amy Phillips in preparing the final manuscript for printing and of Kathy Zeigler for proofreading the final copy.

Chapter 1

Planning Perspectives

You've got to come up with a plan. You can't wish things will get better.

—John F. Welch
CEO, General Electric

PLANNING PERSPECTIVE

All organizations do at least some planning even if it is largely informal and even largely unintentional. One writer states, "planning has to be defined by the *process* it represents" (Mintzberg, 1994). The process is largely informal in many institutions which means it is also incremental (each decision builds upon prior planning decisions). Informal planning, however, leads to misunderstandings because there are few records of planning decisions which have been made, planning efforts are sporadic, and it is likely that the effort will not result in a completed plan. There is also no system of follow-through. Informal planning is not likely to be comprehensively implemented. Effective planning is a disciplined process.

If we have authority and responsibility in an institution (regardless of whether administrative, faculty, or staff), we find ourselves observing how the present is evolving into the future and how things we would like to see happen are sometimes (and sometimes not) becoming a part of that future. The extent to which we think about such things is the extent to which we are beginning the planning process. Planning begins with (1) the assumption that there is a future, and that (2) maybe it should be different than the present, along with (3) realizing that we can do something about that future, and then (4) resolving that we will take action. Let's look at these four concepts.

All of us know that there is a future. Not all of us care about the future. Most of us know that it will be at least a little different from the present even if we do nothing to bring about the difference. Many of us are content to have the fascinating future be created by others and are willing to sit back and take in the benefits of what that future might bring. Part of this is due to the expectation that the future will be better than the present. We point to the progress of this century. If we are from the United States or Canada, we look at how inventions, the standard of living, health care, and other improvements have come about without much effort on our part. Why mess up a good thing? If we continue as we have for the past 40 years and continue to avoid a major war, we expect prosperity, stability, conveniences, better health, more wealth, and most other things that we value. In short, why plan when the world is getting better every day without a planning effort on our part?

The second concept is determining whether we want the future to be different from the present and the past. Some of us say why bother? Some of us, on the other hand, find the future possibilities exciting. We consider ways in which the future will be different due to major forces such as the increased role of technology and technological breakthroughs, or the opportunities we face due to a strong economy and political freedom that encourage entrepreneurial and creative activities on our part and which work toward fulfilling our urges and interests.

The third concept is realizing that we can do something about that future. This requires vision, the ability to dream, to visualize what could happen if the right efforts take place. Affecting the future begins with an understanding that the future is capable of being different from the present and that you and others around you can help shape that future. It must include the understanding that the present is going to change anyway. The rapid rate of change in society today is changing private higher education. Not all of that change is good for private higher education. Who and what should determine the future of private higher education? Should we leave it to society as a whole, a few leadership institutions, a few courageous leaders who will point the way? In visualizing the future, we need to be attentive to society, the leader institutions, and the individual leaders, but we have the option of creating our own destiny, limited primarily by our vision of what we would like the future to be.

And then we have the fourth concept, resolving that we will take action to affect that future. This is the tough one. This means taking action based upon our vision of what we would like the future to be. The number of people who are seriously in this category on a consistent basis is relatively small. The need for positive people in this category is very high. The impact of people in this category is that they are the ones who shape the world. These are the people who lead the world and create the interesting setting in which the rest of us live. The great opportunity is that each of us can decide whether we want to be in this category. There are no elections, no dues to pay, just leadership to exert and then to enjoy the satisfaction that comes from seeing something happen that has come about because of our leadership and the leadership of others.

STARTING THE PROCESS

Planning begins with someone thinking that strategic planning is important for this institution. Someone or a group decides that the effort that might be exerted would produce outcomes which would be worthwhile. We still might think that planning as a concept sounds worthwhile, but what could it do for our institution? If you are struggling with any of the following problems or questions, planning could be very important to you:

- Why is there so much confusion among our faculty, staff, and/or students about what we are trying to accomplish?
- Why is there so much dissension and disagreement in this institution?
- Why is there such a high turnover of people in our college, especially in leadership positions?
- Why did we spend money on new services when they are not being used?
- As an administrator or faculty member, why am I working 12 hours a day, and can never keep up?

- Why have we failed on a number of projects and programs?
- Why has our funding dropped off?
- Why does this institution lack enthusiasm?
- Why has the Board asked me (or any key person) to resign after everything I (they) have put into this institution?

If you are wrestling with any of these questions, the answer might be that your institution lacks effective strategic planning. And you would be in good company. Consider the recent sagas of such diverse private educational institutions as the University of Bridgeport (Wallingford and Berger, 1993), Millikin University (Cope, 1987), and Atlantic Baptist College (McKinnon, 1994). What do these organizations have in common? They are all private colleges or universities that have used strategic planning as they faced up to and successfully overcame external threats to their well-being including declining memberships or enrollments and serious revenue shortfalls.

In the past, traditional business enterprises were the primary users of strategic planning. Increasingly, however, educational institutions have begun to apply strategic planning concepts to improve the effectiveness of their operations. And, as we shall see, a fundamental part of strategic planning is the team-building approach of developing leaders and having people involved in the development and implementation of the plan.

PLANNING IS IMPORTANT

Planning as part of the management process is crucial to the success of any institution. This is especially true for private colleges, universities, and graduate schools. However, the increasing volatility of the environments in which all organizations, including both for-profit and not-for-profit institutions, must function has forced major changes in the scope of the planning process. No longer will it suffice simply to lay plans for internal operations. To adapt to ever-changing environmental forces, organizations have moved to strategic planning with its greater emphasis on stretching the organization to maintain a proper fit between it and the demands of both its external environment and its internal culture. Today, strategy formulation and implementation (parts of the strategic planning process) are essential for effective performance of every college, university, seminary, technical school, or other part of higher education.

Out of a large number of decisions made by an institution or by an individual administrator, there are a handful of critical ones that can significantly impact the future of the institution or its leader. In some cases it is the failure to make a needed decision which will impact the institution. These strategic decisions require careful identification and thoughtful consideration. This is the nature of the role of strategic planning.

STRATEGIC THINKING

Strategic thinking is akin to critical thinking, a familiar concept in higher education. Traditionally, critical thinking has been identified with the field of logic and the mental ability to reason in the abstract. Today, critical thinking is an essential element of most disciplines including management, leadership, and strategic planning. Strategic thinking might be explained as focusing on higher level learning and more complex thinking abilities. Thus, categories in the cognitive domain such as analysis, synthesis, and evaluation are rich fields for critical thinking. However, our focus is that of strategic planning in a practical and applied context. Therefore, we must direct critical thinking beyond knowledge within a discipline to application:

- Between disciplines
- To real-world predictable problems
- To real-world unpredictable problems

Strategic thinking also emphasizes:

- Asking and seeking answers to penetrating questions which affect survival of the organization
- Scanning the environment, both external and internal, for unique ways of "doing more with less at higher quality"

A leader who thinks strategically will focus on the following:

- Conceptualize direction-setting actions for the organization
- Identify areas of change that will impact the vision, mission, and overall goals of the institution
- Look at the big picture–across traditional boundaries and beyond the next two to three years
- Emphasize the why and the how (instead of what) of strategy design and implementation
- Search for the best competitive advantage, or best competitive position relative to other key institutions which may target similar student markets and donors

Strategic thinking emphasizes development and implementation of organization-wide or overall strategies with accountability toward effectiveness, efficiency, and quality in mind.

Perspectives of strategic thinking can be illustrated with the question, "Who are the two most important persons responsible for the success of an airplane's flight?" Typical responses would be:

- the pilot and the navigator, or
- the pilot and the maintenance supervisor, or
- the pilot and the air traffic controller, or
- the pilot and the flight engineer.

All of these responses recognize the day-to-day hands-on importance of the pilot. They all introduce one of several other important support or auxiliary functionaries to the answer. However, each of these segmented responses ignores the one person who is perhaps the single most important individual to the ultimate success of the airplane–the designer. Perhaps the pilot and the designer are the two individuals most important to the success of an airplane's flight–because of the pilot's day-to-day responsibilities in commanding the craft and the designer's ability to create a concept that can be economically constructed, easily operated by any normally competent flight crew, and safely maintained by the ground crew.

Most contemporary administrators of private institutions perceive themselves as the "pilots" of their institutions: taking off, landing, conferring with the navigator, and communicating with the air traffic controller. They generally view themselves as the chief hands-on operational managers. However, what has been most lacking in these institutions in the past few years has been an appreciation for the strategic planning viewpoint. There is a need for more emphasis on an integrated "designer-pilot" approach to operating an educational venture. A well-conceived, continuously updated strategic planning system can facilitate this emphasis.

An institution without a strategic planning perspective faces a tough situation. Instead of moving steadily toward its goals, the institution will continually swerve off course due to the endless supply of distractions that can prevent an institution from pursuing its vision and mission. Thus, strategic planning is one of the keys to success of any undertaking, and nowhere is it more important than in private higher education.

WHAT IS PLANNING?

Planning might be defined as a managerial activity which involves determining your fundamental mission as an institution, analyzing the external environment and the internal culture (including its underlying value system), setting objectives, deciding on a specific action plan needed to reach the objectives, and then adapting the original plan as feedback on results is received. This process should be distinguished from the plan itself, which is a written document containing the results of the planning process. The plan is a written statement of what is to be done and how it is to be done. Planning is a continuous process which both precedes and follows other functions. Plans are made and executed and results are used to make new plans as the process continues.

TYPES OF PLANS

There are many types of plans but most can be categorized as either *strategic* or *tactical*. Strategic plans cover a long period of time and might be referred to as *long-term plans*. They are broad in scope and basically answer the question of how an institution is to commit its resources over the next five to ten years in order to accomplish its mission. Strategic plans are altered on a periodic basis (often annually) to reflect changes in the external environment or internal culture and sometimes the overall direction of the institution.

Tactical plans cover a short time period, usually a year or less. They are often referred to as *short-term* or *action plans*. They specify what is to be done in a given period of time to either address a specific issue (threat or opportunity) or move the institution toward its long-term objectives as recorded in a strategic plan. In other words, what we do this year (short term and tactical) needs to be tied to where we want to be five to ten years in the future (long term and strategic). In higher education, an example of a tactical plan is one that plans and implements a departmental project (such as a research project or the development of a new course).

Most institutions that have been involved in planning have focused on tactical short-term rather than strategic long-term planning. This is better than not planning at all, but it also means each year's plan is not related to anything long-term in nature and usually falls short of moving the institution to where it wants to be in the future.

Planning is required for programs and events as well as for whole institutions. A *program* is a large set of activities involving a whole area of an institution's capabilities, such as planning for a new adult-oriented degree completion program, a new degree program at the master's level, or the decision of a K-8 school system to add a high school. Planning for programs involves:

1. Dividing the total set of activities into meaningful parts.
2. Assigning planning responsibility for each part to appropriate people.
3. Assigning target dates for completion of plans.
4. Determining and allocating the resources needed for each part.

Each major program or department within an institution should have a strategic plan in place to provide a blueprint for the program over time.

An *event* is generally a project of less scope and complexity. It is also not likely to be repeated on a regular basis. An event might be a part of a broader program or it might be self-contained. Even when it is a one-time event, planning is an essential element to accomplish the objectives of the project and coordinate the activities which make up the event. For example, a plan to have a fundraiser for a new field house or library would be an example of a project plan.

PRIVATE HIGHER EDUCATION

Most institutions of private higher education are not-for-profit. However, there are some for-profit colleges and universities, and they are now able to achieve regional accreditation. The typical profit-seeking college or university relies almost solely on the sale of its services to the public for its revenue. The not-for-profit college or university also relies upon gifts and contributions for much of its revenue, and institutions such as research universities rely upon government and private research grants. In some cases there are special programs that are government funded. Let's explore the differences between these three types of institutions within higher education.

Almost all institutions can be classified into three types:

1. Private for-profit or proprietary educational firms. These firms provide educational services in the marketplace with the primary mission of earning a profit from operations. Such institutions are often of a very high quality level. They are primarily tuition driven; as a minimum they have a higher percentage of total revenue derived from tuition and fees than not-for-profit institutions.
2. Private not-for-profit educational institutions. This type of organization is by far the most common college, university, or other private school legal form. In serving the public, these institutions typically rely heavily on endowments, gifts, and contributions, in addition to the tuition and fee revenue they might generate and from the sale of auxiliary goods and services. They vary considerably in purpose and scope from single purpose institutions (such as Fuller Seminary in California) to comprehensive universities (such as Vanderbilt University in Tennessee).

3. Public (government-supported) universities and colleges. Funded by taxes, these are created by law at the federal, state, and local levels to provide higher education services for the general public. Most of these institutions are created by the states although the state will sometimes operate the institution through a local board created by state law. Increasingly, this type of institution is directly competing for gifts and grants, a factor private higher education must include in its strategic planning. Most public institutions are state controlled, although in some cases with local boards of control (or advisory) such as in some community college systems. The tendency today is to decrease federal and local involvement (decline of the city university, for example) in higher education and to centralize control at the state level (an example is the action by the state of Minnesota to place all public higher education, and including community colleges but excepting the University of Minnesota, under one state board).

This book is designed specifically for private colleges, universities, seminaries, and graduate schools (not-for-profit and for-profit), and any other form of private higher education. However, we intend much of what is said in these pages to have relevance for the private for-profit and private not-for-profit organizations described above, such as independent schools and academies (kindergarten through grade 12), church-related schools and academies (kindergarten through grade 12), private colleges and universities, and proprietary schools and institutes.

DATA SOURCES

Several data sources, both governmental and private, develop classification categories for institutions of higher education. For example, many data banks use the following institutional types as identified by the Carnegie Commission:

- Research Universities I
- Research Universities II
- Doctorate Granting Universities I

- Doctorate Granting Universities II
- Comprehensive Universities and Colleges I
- Comprehensive Universities and Colleges II
- Liberal Arts Colleges I
- Liberal Arts Colleges II
- Two-Year Junior Colleges
- Theological Seminaries, Bible Colleges, and other institutions offering degrees in religion
- Schools of Engineering and Technology
- Schools of Business and Management

These classifications are not hard-and-fast or absolute, but are based on program emphasis as indicated by the number of degrees awarded by field and level.

ADVANTAGES OF PLANNING FOR PRIVATE HIGHER EDUCATION

Why should an institution devote time to planning? Consider the following questions:

- "Do you know where you are going and how you are going to get there?"
- "Does everyone in the organization (all the stakeholders) know what you are trying to accomplish?"
- "Do all the stakeholders know what is expected of them?"

If the answer to any of these is "no" or "I'm not sure," then the institution needs to develop a strategic plan with as many people involved as possible. And it has never been more crucial in the dynamic environment your college or university faces. Strategic planning can guide your organization through decision making and actions that will determine whether the institution prospers, survives, or fails.

Strategic planning should be considered for a higher education institution for several reasons:

1. To improve performance toward meeting the mission statement,
2. To improve performance toward increasing the academic standing of the institution,

3. To increase accomplishments with the same or lower level of resources,
4. To clarify the future direction of the institution,
5. To solve major problems (threats) or address significant opportunities facing the institution,
6. To meet the requirements of accreditation or a government agency,
7. To provide an opportunity for leadership such as at the time of the appointment of a new president, and
8. To bring the college/university community together in an effort being done cooperatively.

In many small colleges, administrators might object to planning, thinking that it makes no sense for them since they are only a small organization and everyone associated knows what happened in the past year and what is likely to happen in the coming year. Another objection often voiced is that there is no time for planning. A third objection is that there are not enough resources to allow for planning.

All these objections actually point out the necessity for planning even in the small institution. The fact that there is no strategic plan might be a key reason that outside organizations will not show interest in helping the institution with financial resources in the form of gifts or grants. Even a small college might have a sizable budget, making it imperative to have a plan as to where the organization is heading. The feeling that there is no time for planning might seem accurate, but probably simply reflects the fact that the lack of planning in the past has left insufficient time for attention to such necessities. It could also infer the lack of higher education experience by the administrative staff of the institution. Finally, the argument that there are insufficient resources should justify the role of planning in order to obtain the maximum benefit from those resources being used in the organization.

In the medium or large institution, the arguments against planning might take a different form—complexity of the institution causing it to have many different priorities at the same time, growing enrollment and growing endowment and other income, stable leadership, stable faculty and programs, a beautiful campus. All of these can make an institution complacent. We are doing fine as we are.

Plus, we are very busy and strategic planning will take time from those who are involved in leading the institution today.

Strategic planning in the medium or large private institution is the setting of those priorities among the various elements within the institution which are competing. Without strategic planning, those decisions tend to get made in a weekly president's cabinet meeting, or in the budget committee. As a general rule, other than event planning (see prior definition), planning should not be done in a budget committee. A budget committee should be allocating financial resources according to a plan made by a different group; that is, the strategic plan drives the budget–not the other way around. When budget committees plan for an institution, they tend to give priority to those activities which will benefit a balanced budget or will reduce expenses and increase revenue in the short run.

The other factors given for not planning in a medium or large private institution given above include growing enrollment and other factors indicating both growth and stability (administration and faculty). The thinking might be, if we can grow and prosper without planning, why do it? The response is that with strategic planning there will be considerations about where to grow, and how these good times can be used to become the institution we envision. Tomorrow will not be a duplicate of today without planning. The world around us is changing too rapidly. Only through strategic planning will the medium or large private institution be able to fully take advantage of the factors working for them today to forge the future that is desired.

Thus, planning is a critical element in the success of any college or university. The arguments for planning vary from one type of institution to another, but all private higher education institutions need to engage themselves in a process of strategic planning.

Planning has many advantages. For example, it helps administrators adapt to changing environments, take advantage of opportunities created by change, reach agreements on major issues, and place responsibility more precisely. It also gives a sense of direction to staff members as well as providing a basis for gaining their commitment. The sense of vision that can be provided in a well-written plan also instills a sense of loyalty in organization members or constituents.

A private institution can benefit from the planning process because it is a systematic, continuing process that allows it to:

1. Assess its market position. This involves what is termed a *SWOT* analysis–examining the institution's internal *S*trengths and *W*eaknesses and external *O*pportunities and *T*hreats. Without explicit planning these elements might go unrecognized.
2. Establish goals, objectives, priorities, and strategies to be completed within specified time periods. Planning will enable the institution to assess accomplishment of the goals that are set and will help motivate staff and volunteers to work together to achieve shared goals.
3. Achieve greater staff and member commitment and teamwork aimed at meeting challenges and solving problems presented by changing conditions.
4. Muster its resources to meet these changes through anticipation and preparation.
5. Provide protective benefits resulting from reduced chances for error in decision making.
6. Provide positive benefits in the form of increased success in reaching institutional objectives, overall goals, and the mission itself.

Higher education leaders cannot control the future, but they should attempt to identify and isolate present actions and to forecast how results from actions taken now can be expected to influence the future. The primary mission of planning, then, is to see that current programs and findings can be used to increase the chances of achieving the mission statement and the specific strategies and Key Result Areas; that is, to increase the chances of making better decisions today that affect tomorrow's performance. Key Result Areas, as used in this book, are major focus areas in strategic planning. Each Key Result Area reflects major change in one segment of the institution. There are likely to be several objectives in each Key Result Area.

Unless planning improves focus and the attainment of the mission statement, it is not worthwhile. Thus, to have an institution that looks forward to the future and tries to stay alive and prosper in a changing environment, there must be active, vigorous, continuous, and creative planning. Otherwise, an institution will only react to its external environment and internal culture.

Some institutions and their leaders who plan poorly, if at all, constantly devote their energies to solving problems that would not have existed, or at least would be much less serious, with planning. Thus they spend their time fighting fires rather than practicing fire prevention.

At the same time, every institution has opportunities. Strategic planning allows the institution to take advantage of such opportunities through strategic use of resources and a mindset that is oriented toward future possibilities.

Strategic planning can become a means of renewal in the life of an organization if the following five significant points (McKinnon, 1994) about planning are remembered:

1. A unified mission can be achieved only when all segments of the institution see themselves as part of a larger whole with focused goals/objectives.
2. Isolated individual decisions and commitments often influence future plans, even when they are not intended to do so.
3. When careful planning is lacking, groups in the institution often become competitive with one another and duplicate one anothers' work.
4. Without coordinated planning, groups in the institution might come to feel they are ends in themselves and lose their sense of perspective in relation to the organization.
5. The magnitude of the tasks facing an institution demand long-range planning.

PLANNING'S PLACE IN PRIVATE HIGHER EDUCATION

We are now ready to discuss who does the planning, or the place of planning in an institution. Obviously, all leaders engage in planning to some degree. As a general rule, the larger the institution becomes, the more the primary planning activities become associated with groups of people as opposed to individuals such as the president and one or two advisors.

Many larger institutions develop a planning team and/or a planning staff. Organizations set up such a planning team and/or staff for one or more of the following reasons:

1. *Planning takes time.* A planning team can reduce the workload of individual staff or members by sharing the work to be done in the planning process.
2. *Planning takes coordination.* A planning team can help integrate and coordinate the planning activities of individual staff.
3. *Planning takes expertise.* A planning team can bring to a particular problem more tools and techniques than any single individual.
4. *Planning takes objectivity.* A planning team can take a broader view than one individual and go beyond specific projects and particular organizational departments.

A planning team generally has three basic areas of responsibility. First, it assists administrators in developing goals, strategies, and policies for the institution. The planning team facilitates this process by scanning and monitoring the institution's environment. A second major responsibility of the planning team is to coordinate the planning of different levels and units within the institution. Finally, the planning team acts as an organizational resource for administrators who lack expertise in planning.

A major caution, however, is that no institution, regardless of size or other characteristics, should delegate strategic planning to a planning team alone. Strategic planning, in order to be appropriate and effective, must be the commitment from the board, the president, and all other key players on a campus including administrators, staff, and faculty.

In smaller institutions, planning and execution must usually be carried out by the same people. The greatest challenge is setting aside time for planning in the midst of all the other activities needed on a day-to-day basis. This will happen, particularly in a small institution, if the president makes a commitment to strategic planning that is evident to everyone on the campus, on the board, and to the students, faculty, and community.

In large institutions, the challenge is in effective communication to those who are not directly part of the planning process so that they are aware of the process going on and also made aware of their ability to affect that process. The process could become a mechanical one without leadership and thus not very effective. A bureaucratic staff in planning could take the place of widespread involvement of the stakeholders.

In institutions of any size, the president is a key figure. Where the president is aloof from the process, planning will never be fully successful. The president must signal to the constituencies that planning is important and that it will play a significant role in the future of the institution. The president could be a member of the planning team, even its chair. But the president must, as a minimum, be very aware of the planning process through periodic updates, and must make support of the planning process a very visible part of the presidency. It is essential that actions by the president that will affect the future be consistent with the effort coming from a strategic planning effort. Presidents cannot plan by themselves while appointing a planning team to go through the motions of planning.

Wise presidents see strategic planning as an opportunity to provide leadership within the institution. One reason is that it creates the scenario in which there is meaningful dialogue with the key leaders on campus. Second, it puts the important issues of the campus on the table where the president can have some impact. The president who cannot effectively plan in the institution he or she leads will be unable to provide leadership in other areas of the institution and will thus be only partially effective at best. In Chapter 4 on organizational culture, we talk about leadership as being tied to the ability to affect the culture of a campus. Likewise, leadership is tied to the ability to bring about effective strategic planning.

Persons other than the president within an institution who are devoted to seeing effective planning take place are reminded that their ability to bring about such planning is closely related to their ability to bring the president of the institution into the process. Even if the president plays only a nominal role in the process of planning, it is the president who will determine directly or indirectly whether the plan itself is taken seriously as decisions are being made about the future of the institution each day.

RESISTANCE TO THE PLANNING PROCESS

There are four main reasons why planning does not get done in institutions today: (1) administrators lack training, (2) many perceive it as irrelevant, (3) problems can occur in implementation, and (4) lack of leadership from the president.

Lack of Management Preparation/Involvement

Many institutions are small with an even smaller core of active leaders. The educational background and experience of the leaders of these organizations varies widely. Those with prior management experience often possess a proactive, can-do attitude and want to spend their time performing hands-on functions with which they are comfortable. Furthermore, many institutions cannot or do not draw on a pool of volunteers or consultants with management training or skills. As such, the refinement of the mission statement, the development of Key Result Areas, setting objectives, and assembling action plans and other planning functions are largely neglected or ignored.

Closely related to ignoring the potential of planning is the failure to involve key people in the strategic planning process. While the planning team cannot involve everyone, the team can in turn involve every member of the campus constituency in the overall planning process. Only through involvement will there be a sense of this planning being "my planning and therefore something I want to see placed in effect." Likewise, as stated above, involvement must include the president of the institution. Similarly, vice presidents who are not consulted or given an opportunity to participate in the strategic planning process are in a position of making sure that the positive parts of the plan are not achieved. Some small colleges have a tradition of little involvement for faculty. To continue that tradition in the strategic planning process is a major error. It ignores a valuable resource within the institution for ideas and does not take into account the important role of faculty in making the strategic plan unfold over a period of time.

Very few college administrators, faculty, or staff have any professional training or detailed knowledge of effective planning. In a large institution there could be some people with such expertise who can guide others. Small institutions are not likely to have such persons on their staff. Even presidents are rarely trained in strategic planning. Presidents tend to be selected on the basis of their ability to raise funds and handle crises, their close identification with a sizable constituency (such as a church or other religious body), or because of their personal/social skills (pleasing personality and ability to smile). Few are chosen due to their academic knowledge, ability, or interests. As a result, planning is often a challenge for a president who has little knowledge or experience with institutional planning and is therefore unaware or skeptical of its possibilities.

To balance the lack of preparation of presidents and others in the area of planning, the Kellogg Foundation in the 1960s and 1970s played a significant role in preparing community college presidents and other administrators for the important tasks they were about to assume. Institutions today have the option of seeking consulting assistance from firms which can help private institutions go through the planning process. Another option is to seek out workshops or institutes which have strategic planning included in the agenda. Nonetheless, this often leaves the initiative with other segments of the higher education community, such as accrediting bodies and associations, which have taken more of a leadership role in urging strategic planning in recent years. Some inactivity on the part of institutions has led to state agencies becoming more active in controlling private higher education within the state.

Planning Is Thought to Be Irrelevant

Developing Key Result Areas and objectives with corresponding strategies has been largely neglected or purposely avoided by many institutions. This reluctance to plan stems from the fact that many view the application of strategic planning as irrelevant. Some have felt that because the environment in which institutions work changes so rapidly, laying out formal plans and objectives is a useless endeavor. With this view, constantly shifting environmental demands outside the educational institution's control can make objectives obsolete, the reasoning goes, before they become official documents of the institution, so why develop them at all? Unfortunately, the consequence of this perspective is a leadership doomed to reactionary, piecemeal approaches to environmental demands, often resulting in less than desirable performance. It means accepting the future created by others.

Other strategic goal setting challenges in colleges and universities might color attitudes against planning. Many colleges and universities are church-oriented institutions, for example. Church organizations might control the institution or have a major impact on its role and direction making the process of strategic planning difficult and limited in effect. A set of demands and expectations from a major donor might be very similar. It is not always clear that strategic planning will result in pleasing that church organization or donor.

Further, professionals such as faculty tend to be wed more to their profession and less to the organization and its objectives. This seems to be true more with the larger institution because of its larger array of specific loyalties outside the institution. The problem is particularly evident when, in the professionals' views, the organization's goals conflict with those of their profession.

Finally, colleges and universities face the daunting task of trying to serve the often varying interests of their students, faculty and staff, and funding sources. Thus, there is often a wide range of values within any one institution's culture—such a wide range that consensus is difficult at best, particularly in a comprehensive university. Some might say that the results of strategic planning would serve to please only some constituencies while disappointing others. The strategy could be that it is better to be vague than risk losing participation and financial support. But this approach is one of risk avoidance rather than one of opportunity taking and threat elimination.

Implementation Problems

Although there is much academic and theoretical support for planning, the actual implementation of it often runs aground on the shores of operational reality. Even among very progressive institutions, significant resistance to planning might be found. Some of the most common arguments against it are:

1. Planning is not sufficiently action-oriented.
2. Planning takes too much time; we are too busy to plan.
3. Planning becomes an end, not just a means to an end.
4. Planning never ends up being carried out exactly as intended.

Many of these arguments stem from the same kind of thinking that would say that the pilot was the most important person in the success of an airplane's flight, referring back to the airplane/designer analogy. The feeling that planning is not "hands-on" and related to the important day-to-day operations of the institution is frequently heard. However, this point of view is short-sighted in terms of long-run success. Planning is not just for dreamers; in fact, it lets the institution's administrative team determine what can be done today to accomplish or avoid some future circumstance.

Planning sometimes becomes an end in the minds of some users. This is particularly true when established solely as a committee responsibility within an organization. A committee can facilitate the strategic planning process, but the process will not be a dynamic life-blood activity of the organization without the ongoing involvement of all the stakeholders in the institution.

President Eisenhower has been widely quoted as saying, "Plans are nothing, planning is everything." The truth he expressed was that the actual plan itself was not the end itself, but that the process of planning—developing futuristic scenarios, evaluating the external environment and the internal culture, assessing internal strengths and capabilities, revising objectives and action plans—is the organizational dialogue that is the most important. This dialogue ideally breaks down barriers to communication, exposes blind spots to the light, tests logic, and measures the environment and culture; it determines feasibility as well.

Planning does not depend on complete forecasting accuracy to be useful. In sports, even the very best game plans are often adapted as play goes on. Yet coaches continue to develop game plans with each new opponent. They understand that the importance of planning is to keep the institution moving in the right direction even if the finer points of the plan are constantly being adjusted to new circumstances (the changing circumstance might be strategic planning being done by a competing institution). And in making these adjustments, a variety of futuristic alternatives or scenarios can be very helpful in establishing planning parameters. Often a best-case, most-likely-case, and worst-case approach is used.

Lack of Leadership from the President

Some small institutions' presidents come from backgrounds other than higher education such as ministry, government service, or for-profit business, which might make them uncomfortable working in cooperative activities with other key people on campus, such as faculty. Lack of experience as a president could cause a new president to "hold the cards close to the chest" so as not to reveal insecurities about the role. A president might have few clues as to the future direction of the institution and be concerned about others learning about this indefiniteness. The effective president is not usually the one who makes waves in higher education or the institution, but instead is a person who can quietly and effectively work with others to forge an appropriate future for the institution.

A research study of the best-managed Christian, liberal arts colleges in the United States revealed a number of characteristics of presidents in the colleges considered by those interviewed to be the best managed. The ten colleges most frequently mentioned as being best managed were located around the United States and had many characteristics they did not share. The one characteristic they did share was a president who articulated the mission and worked well with others as a team leader to find ways to implement this mission (Oosting, 1996).

Summary–Resistance to the Planning Process

After looking at the four reasons given above for resistance to the planning process, the reader can consider which of these reasons, if any, exist on his or her campus. The next step is to determine how to address the resistance effectively. In spite of these reasons for resisting the planning process, each institution is urged to overcome the reasons that exist because the advantages of planning far outweigh any disadvantages. Planning not only should be done but must be done if an institution is to achieve a sizable portion of its mission.

REVENUE SOURCE INFLUENCES ON PLANNING

Another factor influencing whether strategic planning will occur is the adequacy of institutional funding. Executives of any business enterprise must be concerned about continuous, adequate sources of revenue for the survival of their businesses. Traditional businesses have a straightforward objective. They can focus on pleasing the customer. For the leader of a private higher education institution, however, these concerns are different and possibly more complex.

For many institutions, the focus on exactly who the customer is might become fuzzy. This is due to the fact that the recipient of an institution's services might not be the same person who directly pays the bill. Low income students' tuition is paid directly by a third party, the federal government and/or state government. Students with high scholarship potential receive merit scholarships from a variety of institutional or outside sources. Public universities are largely funded by state legislatures. Many schools, colleges, and universities have unrestricted endowments which finance some of the institution's overhead expenses.

Any college or university—not-for-profit or proprietary—tends to give serious attention to the desires of those who foot the bill. And to the extent that there is a funding sponsor providing financial support for the client, the client's influence over the institution's goals and performance might be weakened.

One consequence of intervening sources of funding for institutions is the tendency to ignore the client's needs in favor of the funding sponsor's demands where the two conflict. In attempts to satisfy both parties, institutions might avoid goal setting or develop goals that are vague at best.

Unfortunately, highly generalized goals have their performance shortcomings. In contrast, there is plenty of evidence that goals which are relatively specific and measurable, wherever possible, support higher performance in organizations.

The message for institutions is that the strategic planning process can provide the understandable goals they need. It does this by systematically considering the expectations of all those who hold a stake in the effectiveness of the institution's operation. Thus strategic planning is the vehicle that can produce goals which are defined as clearly as possible toward the end of meeting both the client's needs and the scrutiny of the sponsor.

THE GREATEST NEEDS OF TODAY'S PRIVATE COLLEGES AND UNIVERSITIES

Every president of a private college or university would be able to readily respond to the question of what the greatest needs of today's private colleges and universities might be. The lists would not be identical but some similarities would appear. The need for adequate funding, quality learning, and public understanding and acceptance would make most lists.

Strategic planning offers a means by which the list of needs can be developed by a cross section of the campus community. Strategic planning also offers then a means of possible realization of success in meeting those needs. Presidents, faculties, deans, and staff all need to come to understand that success in meeting these needs, even identifying the needs that are most pressing, will come by working together in a collaborative effort that represents institutional strategic planning rather than planning by only one of the persons or groups within the institution. By working together there is a Gestalt effect which brings a net effect that is greater than the sum of the parts.

Needs are best identified by a group that represents the various constituencies within and outside of the institution. Strategic planning must begin by identifying the mission and the specific needs in realizing that mission. Only then can the process begin to bring about a different institution.

There seems to be a widespread notion that growth is the only barometer of institutional success, but we prefer to offer a different criteria for success. Far greater than success in reaching numerical growth goals and then maintaining that number, institutions should reach for excellence. It is not as important that we do many things for many people as it is that whatever we do, we do it with excellence (see Johnston, 1996, for further development of this thought). Rather than ask the question of how many should be involved in the planning process, we suggest that institutions ask the question of how well it can be done (and not attempt to do what cannot be done by the institution perceived to be the model). As to growth and becoming larger, we hold that there is no optimum size for all institutions. Instead, size should be related to excellence in achieving the mission statement for those people the institution exists to serve, however large or small the group might be.

One of the greatest needs in institutions of higher learning is for leadership. Untapped leadership exists in many institutions. But we believe the greatest problems holding back these leaders–and the organizations they serve–involve the need for proactive leaders at all levels within an institution who understand and accept the mission, will consider the vision in future shaping of the institution, and are willing to develop Key Result Areas and action plans which assign responsibilities for accomplishing objectives on a timely basis with the needed resources for implementation.

Maybe the missing ingredient for would-be leaders is often the courage factor. The courage factor is what allows an individual to act upon his or her dreams, mission, and objectives. Institutions as well as the individuals within it need to have sufficient courage to make leadership work. How does a person and an institution gain courage? We believe it comes from attention to vision and mission and getting excited about implementing the vision and mission. Excitement gives institutions and persons the courage to act. There is much to be excited about in private higher education today. Getting involved in helping an institution reach its mission could cause a person to become excited. The greater the number of people who are excited, the greater the courage factor that exists.

Institutions need to prepare their people for strategic planning. Without training and knowledge in the area of planning and management, an institution has placed a ceiling on excellence. No organization can get any bigger than the capacity of its managers to manage. The hindrance is not in the lack of needs of the constituent groups, because they are always there. Nor is it the organization's reputation or location; rather, it is simply the keys to effective management including effective strategic planning involving the development of an agreed upon mission statement, appropriate institutional structure, involvement of the right people who are motivated and trained, leadership with a sufficient courage factor, and evaluation and control to ensure that the mission is in fact being implemented.

SUGGESTED AREAS OF INSTITUTIONAL NEED

While we are hesitant to offer a possible list of institutional needs because of the tremendous varying needs of institutions, we present the following to help institutions visualize possible areas of need that they possess. Some possible areas for institutional need are:

1. Ensuring excellence in current activities of the institution.
2. Improving the amount and expanding the types of student learning.
3. Achieving the size that fits our mission.
4. Achieving adequate funding to allow us to fulfill our mission.
5. Encouraging and developing leadership.
6. Attaining the accreditation which is appropriate to our mission.
7. Finding the right faculty and developing the faculty we have.
8. Determining the type and number of staff needed to support our operation and then providing the training and resources to allow them to achieve excellence in what they do.
9. Exploring new avenues of learning including degree completion programs, distance learning, and on-line offerings.
10. Presenting the appropriate public image.
11. Establishing the relationship with possible donors that will encourage their support of the institution.
12. Understanding and coping with government regulations.
13. Achieving positive, proactive communication links on the campus.
14. Bringing about an understanding of our mission within all of our constituencies.
15. Understanding what change would be desirable and having the courage to work toward achieving it.
16. Establishing fiscal responsibility within the institution.
17. Establishing the internal culture which will encourage our fulfillment of our mission.

Each institution will think of needs not in the above list. From the identified needs, an institution can move toward establishing the Key Result Areas as explained in Chapter 6.

THE COMMITMENT TO ACTION

Presidents and their staffs cannot afford to wait until someone creates a big scandal about waste and inefficiency (or some other topic, whether true or not). We need to put our shoulders to the wheel and pay attention to one or more of the areas of institutional need we have identified. If we do not, our institutions will not accomplish nearly as much as they are capable of doing.

Our observation is that many people in college and university leadership positions are reluctant to plan, do not want a plan in writing, or are reluctant to ask for advice. The tendency is to be led by intuition, which is sometimes based on a whim or emotional impulse. This reflects our general American inclination to "hang loose." Probably 75 percent of the profit-making organizations the authors have observed or worked with have the same problem. Yet the 25 percent which have the discipline to plan and manage properly far outperform those that do not. Higher profits, better service, and lower turnover are but a few of the rewards. In private higher education, the same good fortune comes to those colleges and universities which have the discipline to plan and manage effectively.

Many times there is the tendency to say that forces outside our control caused a plan or project to go sour. While sometimes that is the case, too often we are our own worst enemies, holding ourselves back. Many organizational failures can be traced to poor planning, failure to get people involved in the planning, and generally poor management.

Even where that planning is done, we often sense a spirit of extreme urgency. Here the atmosphere is permeated with a "let's go for it—if it is a worthwhile service, it will prosper" mentality. What is the rush? Many institutions need to slow down and plan. Often they have rushed around in circles for the past few years. If it is a worthwhile service, it deserves our best efforts at careful planning. Included in doing our best is using the best planning and management philosophies and techniques available. Of course, strategic planning needs to be timely so that the opportunities from new technology or a demographic change do not pass before we can complete the planning process.

Fundamental to these efforts is effective goal setting. Where planning in education occurs without quantitative goals clearly understood and widely supported, vigorous progress is unlikely and probably impossible. The importance of goal setting is to provide direction and unity of mission, but it must be the organization's goal, for it is not the planners but the organization that will ensure the plan's success. Planning is not easy, but the alternative is for the organization to be tossed to and fro, buffeted by every unforeseen circumstance, and blown off course.

And on a personal level, every leader needs a vision or a dream. Mission statements and vision statements are the vessels through which personal desires can be fulfilled. Yet without a specific mission, a vision remains only a vision.

In a society where many institutions are becoming stagnant, it is imperative that colleges and universities have an expanding vision. Thus, we see creative planning as the institution's best hope for a successful future. Having an agreed upon mission statement and visionary thinking should be basic to operations. Too often planning in institutions has been met with little enthusiasm. The enthusiasm for a plan seldom extends beyond a year unless it involves something tangible, like a new building. Yet no matter how misunderstood and poorly appreciated planning is, it is a major factor in effective performance. The time for strategic planning in your institution is now.

SUMMARY

We have attempted to establish in this introduction our belief that: (1) methods used successfully in industry are applicable to private colleges and universities, (2) there is a place for better strategic planning and effective management in all organizations, (3) many leaders do believe that there is a need for planning, (4) many of the identifiable failures cannot be blamed solely on unforeseen and uncontrollable factors, and (5) the demands of a volatile environment for institutions supports, overall, a growing urgency for the planning concept.

The philosophy of this book is that in order for everyone in the private college or university–students, families, the faculty, the board, the president, and other stakeholders–to be successful, a strategic plan and its effective implementation is desperately needed. If you look at the mistakes of the past, it is obvious that many institutions have floundered because they lack strategic direction. Over years of consulting with these types of organizations, the authors have observed this pattern in a large number of them. If you take the time and effort to study the contents of this book, follow through with others in your institution, and apply the format prescribed here, this is what we believe you can expect:

1. A sense of enthusiasm in the institution;
2. A multiple-year plan in writing to which everyone is committed;
3. A sense of commitment by the entire organization to its overall direction;
4. Clear job duties and responsibilities and thus accountability;
5. Time for the leaders to do what they need to do;
6. Clear and evident improvement in the health and vitality of every member of the organization's staff;
7. Measurable improvement in the personal lives of all those in responsible positions with time for vacations, family, and personal pursuits;
8. The ability to measure very specifically the growth and contribution made by college leaders at the close of their careers;
9. Guaranteed leadership of the institution because a plan is in place in writing and is understood—even more important, a management team and philosophy will be in place to guide the organization into its next era of growth

In this chapter we have presented our belief that the effective performance of leadership and managerial functions in institutions has gained much ground in the last decade. Vast social questions and complex conditions in almost every community now demand the need for good management in higher education.

The next chapter presents an overview of the entire strategic planning process. The subsequent chapters cover each step of the planning process. The theory behind each step is presented and actual examples are given to help you understand that step. Make notes on your own situation as you read. Worksheets found at the ends of the chapters (and collectively in Appendix D) will help you prepare your strategic plan. Also included is our case study, the story of Thorndyke College (Appendix A), as well as a strategic plan outline (Appendix B) and a sample strategic plan (Appendix C). Read on with excitement!

Chapter 2

Overview of Strategic Planning

"Cheshire Puss," she [Alice] began . . . "Would you please tell me which way I ought to go from here?"
"That depends on where you want to get to," said the cat.

—Lewis Carroll
Alice in Wonderland

While the last chapter made the case for why an institution should engage in strategic planning, this chapter presents an overview of the strategic planning process and how to make it work. The areas which are discussed in this chapter are dealt with in more detail in later chapters. The intention here is to provide an introduction to the major components of the strategic planning process.

WHAT IS STRATEGIC PLANNING?

The word "strategic" means "pertaining to strategy." Strategy is derived from the Greek word *strategos* which means generalship, art of the general, or more broadly, leadership. The word "strategic" when used in the context of planning provides a perspective to planning which is long-run in nature and deals with achieving specified end results. Just as military strategy has the objective of the winning of the war, so too, strategic planning has as its goal the achievement of the institution's mission.

Strategic decisions must be differentiated from tactical decisions (see Chapter 1). Strategic decisions outline the overall game plan or approach, while tactical decisions involve implementing various activities (such as events) which are needed to carry out the larger strategy. For example, a college or university which decides to design and implement a degree completion program for adult learners because of shifting preferences among the traditional population is making strategic decisions. Then many other decisions must be made about the faculty and their teaching styles, library access and holdings, student development programs, facilities, and other major details. These all have long-term implications and are therefore strategic in nature.

Then other decisions relating to adjunct faculty, pay policies, library operating hours, and off-site facilities must be made. These are tactical decisions needed to carry out or implement the strategic decision previously made. Thus, strategic decisions provide the overall framework within which the tactical decisions are made. It is critically important that leaders of institutions be able to differentiate between these types of decisions, to identify whether the decision has short-term or long-term implications.

THE STRATEGIC PLANNING PROCESS

The strategic planning process is basically a matching process involving an institution's internal resources and its external opportunities. The objective of this process is to peer through the "strategic window" and identify opportunities for which the individual institution is equipped to take advantage of or respond to in the current or approaching time frame. Thus, the strategic planning process can be defined as *a process which involves matching the institution's capabilities with its threats and opportunities within the context of an institutional mission.*

These opportunities are identified over time and decisions revolve around investing or divesting resources to address these opportunities. The context in which these strategic decisions in the planning process for an institution are made is (1) the external environment, (2) the internal culture of the institution, (3) the mission of the institution, and (4) institution-wide Key Result Areas tied to specific objectives in each of these Areas. This is followed by strategies for implementation of each of the Key Result Areas. Each objective needs to be tied to the Action Plan which details how the objective will be implemented including time frame, person or persons responsible for the implementation, and the resources which will be assigned to the task (human, physical and financial). Strategic planning is the process which ties all these elements together to facilitate the formulation of strategic choices which are internally consistent and then implements these choices. Appendix B presents an outline of a strategic plan.

The successful results of planning described earlier can be achieved through implementing an effective strategic planning process. The following breakdown of this process is a complete outline of a system capable of creating true change in your institution's attitudes as well as in its outcomes.

It is important to recognize at this point what we call "the two Ps." The first "P" means Product: get the plan in writing. The plan must be something you can hold in your hand, a written product of your efforts. If the plan is not in writing, it is called daydreaming. When it is in writing, you are telling yourself and others you are serious about it. The second "P" represents Process: every plan must have maximum input from everyone who will be affected by the implementation of the plan. Those who execute the plan must be involved in construction of the plan in order to gain their commitment. The best way to ensure a plan's failure is to overlook both the product and the process. They are equally important.

While there are many different ways in which an institution can approach the strategic planning process, a systematic approach that carries the institution through a series of integral steps helps focus attention on answering a basic set of questions each institution must answer:

1. *What will we do?* This question focuses attention on the specific needs the institution will try to address.
2. *Who will we do it for?* This question addresses the need for an institution to identify the various groups whose needs will be met.
3. *How will we do what we want to do?* Answering this question forces thinking about the many avenues through which an institution's efforts might be channeled.

The strategic planning process used by an institution must force the institution's leadership to deal with these questions on a continual basis. Ongoing answers to these most fundamental questions allow the institution to continuously adapt over time and do the work it is best suited to do.

Strategic planning is defined as a process that involves completing the six steps shown in Exhibit 2.1. Refer to the "Planning Process Worksheet" at the end of Chapter 2 for specific institutional use as a checklist. The checklist is important because it forces the institution to consider certain questions. As each of the steps requires the people at various institutional levels to discuss, study, and negotiate, the process as a whole fosters a planning mentality. When the six steps are complete, the end result is a strategic plan for the institution specifying why the institution exists, what it is trying to accomplish, and how resources will be utilized to accomplish objectives and fulfill its mission. Let us describe each of the six planning stages.

Defining Mission

The first and probably the most important consideration when developing a strategic plan is to define the mission or the "reason for being" of the institution or any specific part of it.

We suggest that the first step in this process is the development of a vision statement. The vision for an institution is a collection of what the institution might be someday if the dreams and aspirations of those in leadership positions were to reach fruition. The vision might include alternative paths the institution might follow and thus not be internally consistent. The vision might include things that few if any of the leaders think will really come to pass in the way in which it is described today. That might be because of changing technology or changing laws that make it difficult, if not impossible, to have a very clear view of what the details in that part of the vision might be.

There is no failure if some part of the vision never comes to reality. The only failure comes when an institution fails to dream about what might someday be. A vision could reach a generation out into the future and possibly even longer. It could deal with the process of how things will be done (such as the process of how

Exhibit 2.1. Strategic Planning Process

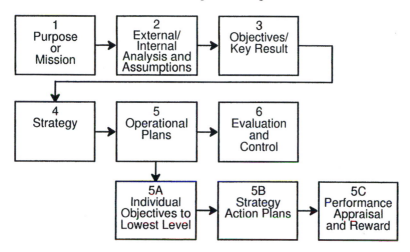

1. Defining an institution's mission and reason for being. An important part of this process is the development of a vision statement that reflects the dreams of what might be someday. Its development can give further focus to the mission statement, which says this is what we endeavor to be today (Chapter 3).
2. Analyzing external environment opportunities and threats and the internal culture of the institution leading to an assessment of the institution's own strengths and weaknesses, and then making assumptions about future operating conditions (Chapters 4 and 5).
3. Developing Key Result Areas that will give a focus to the strategic planning process. There could be some minor areas in which a planning objective is developed that do not tie to a Key Result Area, but the major activity will relate to the Key Result Areas. Prescribing written, specific, and measurable objectives in each of the Key Result Areas plus the minor areas where the proposed action would contribute to the institution's mission (Chapter 6).
4. Developing strategies on how to use available resources to meet objectives (Chapter 7).
5. Developing operational plans that include action plans and strategies/tactics that detail the following (Chapter 7):
   a. The timetable for each strategy and objective.
   b. The assignment of personnel to each strategy and objective (who will be held responsible for making this happen).
   c. The resources (human, physical, and financial) that will be assigned to the task to ensure that it will happen in the form prescribed in the strategic plan and on the timetable stated.
6. Setting up control and evaluation procedures to determine if performance is keeping pace with attainment of objectives and if it is consistent with the defined mission. This is needed both during the process and at set intervals after the process has been completed (Chapter 8).

students will learn 25 years from now) or it might deal with structure (how the institution will be organized or what its facilities will look like). The institution which finds it difficult to develop a vision of its future probably has a limited and uncertain future. If the fires of the present are burning so brightly that the future cannot be contemplated, the strategic planning process probably has little chance of getting the attention it needs to succeed. Strategic planning is the method for keeping the fires of the present from consuming the institution each day.

Establishing an acceptable, workable mission statement can be a difficult process even though it might appear simple. Multiple, often diverse views of the institution's fundamental mission might exist because of the differing perspectives in the numerous constituencies that hold a stake in the performance of the institution. Nevertheless, as Peter Drucker, noted management authority, emphasizes, "The best nonprofits devote a great deal of thought to defining their institution's mission" (Drucker, 1974).

For example, a college or university which defines itself as "an institution to help students gain an education" might be on the right track but will constantly face the need to explain and expand this definition. Does "help" mean offer only financial assistance or does it also include teaching people how to learn? If other services, like health care, are included in the definition, will health services involve only traditional physical care or will other needs be addressed such as psychological counseling or substance abuse treatment? Granted, these things might change as the institution evolves and grows, but thinking through these issues clarifies the mission and also avoids going off on tangential activities which do not fit with what the institution wants to do or be.

The mission statement should be accompanied by the vision statement of what the institution aspires to be. Members should try to visualize what they want the institution to become. If they can see where they are going and have an image of the real mission of the institution, their plans will fall into place more easily. See Chapter 3 on Vision Statements.

A mission statement of what can be accomplished creates the spark and energy for the whole planning and management process. It is important to spend ample time defining this mission statement.

The process should emphasize getting everyone involved in the concept of how the institution should develop. Without a mission statement, people just work day-to-day and tend not to be as productive or willing to go all out because the mission of why they are there is not known or clear.

In addition, a good mission statement not only clarifies what the college or university does, it sets boundaries. It defines what the institution will not do. It helps limit expectations, and that alone can make it a more orderly process when new ideas are proposed, including the dropping of existing programs as well as the introduction of new ones. In such instances, the question of whether the idea fits within the mission must be raised. If it does not, there are two options: don't do it, or change the mission statement. Mission statements should be changed seldom and with deliberation in order to provide stability over a long-term course that is consistent. It is difficult to make a good decision today when the decision maker does not know what the institution will be tomorrow.

There are times, however, when sudden change or planned major change will affect an institution. Sudden change in the financial condition of the institution could raise the specter of closing the institution. In other situations, a merger of two or more institutions, even though planned out over a period of years, will likely mean a rewriting of the mission statement. Many institutions should consider consolidation or merger (or at least closer working ties) during the strategic planning process in order to be more efficient in the use of resources available to the institutions. The strategic planning process is the time to consider merger and consolidation issues.

Analysis and Assumptions

It is vital for the college or university to gauge the external environment and internal culture (see Chapter 4) within which it functions. This should be standard practice for all institutions. The only way we can manage change is to constantly monitor the external environment and internal culture within which we operate. This analysis stage is where we look at the environment external to our institution for potential threats and opportunities, and at our internal culture for strengths and weaknesses.

For example, some "downtown" colleges have faced a dilemma of whether to remain in the downtown area or move to the suburbs. In these instances, the colleges found that their historic location resulted in two significant problems: lack of space to grow and a change in the socioeconomic makeup of the neighborhood. An example of this is San Jose Christian College in San Jose, California. The College has a small campus not far from the downtown area of San Jose. The College appeals to the large local Hispanic population which finds the current campus accessible. However, the College feels the demand to grow in order to serve a greater number of people and, as a result, has considered alternative sites for the campus as well as how to expand in the present site. Other institutions, such as Calvin College in Grand Rapids, Michigan, have sold their campuses and built completely new campuses away from the downtown areas.

Some colleges have established satellite centers in growing parts of their communities. Everybody won! The central campus could serve the needs of those who wished to travel there, while the new locations were built in areas where they could grow and serve additional people. An example is Geneva College in Pennsylvania, which has established the Center for Urban Theological Studies (CUTS) in central Philadelphia.

Many institutions have found it useful to use an analysis framework referred to earlier as a SWOT analysis (introduced in Chapter 1). SWOT is an acronym for Strengths, Weaknesses, Opportunities, and Threats. Strengths and weaknesses refer to elements internal to the institution while opportunities and threats are external to the institution. A detailed SWOT analysis helps a college or university take a good look at the institution's favorable and unfavorable factors with a view toward building on strengths and eliminating or minimizing weaknesses. At the same time, the college or university's leadership must also assess external opportunities which could be pursued and threats which must be dealt with in order to survive.

The next stage is to state your major assumptions about the external environment and the internal culture. These should be made about situations over which you have little or absolutely no control, such as the population and other demographic trends in the external environment, and items in the internal culture that come from the history of the institution. One good place to start is to extend some of the items studied in the external environment analysis. Should this stage appear relatively unimportant in developing a strategic plan, consider this: by not making explicit assumptions you are making one major implicit assumption–things are going to remain the same and nothing that happens is important enough to affect you! Be sure to include in the analysis those things which will affect your strategic planning.

Establishing Key Result Areas and Objectives

Key Result Areas are major aspects of the institution which the strategic plan needs to address. Falling enrollment, inability to end the fiscal year in the black or high faculty turnover are symptoms which suggest a Key Result Area for the strategic planning process. Identifying the major threats to the institution and any opportunity (growing population near the campus, growing value of institution-owned but unused land, or new legislation positively affecting the institution) could be the starting point for developing the Key Result Areas.

While Key Result Areas are an area of activity or a focus, objectives are the description of action that is desired within that Key Result Area. There must be at least one objective for each Key Result Area, but there might be several depending upon the complexity and importance of the Key Result Area. There could also be objectives outside the Key Result Areas in areas that are less complex. Often there will be areas that need to be continued as is, except for one or two fine tuning actions. Those actions can be the subject of an objective.

Often the words "goals" and "targets" are used synonymously with objectives when thinking about long- and short-term objectives. Think of an archer drawing an arrow and aiming directly at a target. The bulls-eye represents exactly where you want to be at a certain point in time. We are calling that an objective, but a particular institution could call it something else as long as there is no confusion about the nomenclature. Leaders will want the whole institution aimed at the same target just as an archer wants the arrow aimed at the target. At the other extreme, an archer who shoots arrows off in any direction is liable to hit almost anything–including the wrong target. People in an institution get confused and disorganized if they do not know where the institution is going or what the target is.

Objectives must be clear, concise, written statements outlining what is to be accomplished in Key Result Areas, over a certain time period and in measurable terms that are consistent with the overall mission of the institution. Objectives are the results desired upon completion of the planning period. Key Result Areas will provide the topic of activity; objectives tell us what we want to do in each area. In the absence of objectives, no sense of direction can be attained in decision making. A basic truism is, "If you don't know where you are going, any road will get you there." In planning, objectives answer one of the basic questions posed in the planning process: Where do we want to go? These objectives become the focal point for strategy decisions.

Another basic function served by objectives is in the evaluation of performance. Objectives in the strategic plan become the yardsticks used to evaluate performance. As will be pointed out later, it is impossible to evaluate performance without some standard against which results can be compared. The objectives become the standards for evaluating performance because they are the statement of results desired by the planners.

Strategy Development

After developing a set of objectives for the Key Result Areas in the time period covered by the strategic plan, the methods or strategies needed to accomplish those objectives must be formulated. This is accomplished in stages.

First, strategies must be developed for implementing each objective. These strategies are developed by examining various alternatives for consideration. Strategy selection during the planning process might need to be refined later. However, it is important to decide upon the alternatives for strategies within the strategic plan. This is based upon the assumption that unless the strategic plan has implementing features within it, it is likely to become just another book on the shelf. Putting off such important decisions as the strategies is simply delaying action that must be taken.

From these specific strategies, an overall strategy can be designed. The grouping of strategies will relate to the Key Result Areas they support. In so doing, strategy becomes the link between objectives and results.

Operational/Action Plans

After these steps have been taken, including strategies developed to meet your objectives and goals, it is time to complete the action plan. The action plan stage is the "doing" stage. Here you hire, fire, add, build, advertise, and complete other activities. How many times has a group of people planned something, become enthusiastic, and then nothing happened? This is usually because they did not complete an action plan to implement their strategy.

Action plans need to be developed in all the areas that are used to support the overall strategy. These include operations, communications, finance, and staffing, as well as all other action areas. Each of these more detailed plans is designed to spell out what needs to happen in a given area to implement the strategic plan.

Supporting the action plan are the individual plans of all members of the institution (as were shown in Steps 5A, 5B, and 5C of Exhibit 2.1). When planning is implemented throughout the institution, everyone becomes involved in developing and setting personal action plans which support the institution's mission and one or more of the specific objectives. The several parts which must be a part of each action plan are:

1. *Who* will be assigned to accomplish the various parts of the action plan? If an item is included within the action plan, there must be a name associated with it to designate who is responsible for making it happen. It needs to be part of that person's performance review for compensation and other rewards and applied consistently to all persons within the institution including vice presidents and the president. While the individual or party responsible could be more than one person, one person must be designated as having the lead responsibility.

2. *When* the action is to take place must be specified in the action plan. A timetable can designate what events are to happen in what sequence. While there should be some flexibility in stat-

ing the time, a statement such as "some time next year" is not adequate. In effect, such a statement means December 31. If that is the intent, it should be stated as December 31. A vague statement of the timetable could lead to misunderstanding about when the action is to take place and thus ill feeling between two or more persons involved in the action plan. A very important part of "when" is sequence. If someone has a responsibility to do something that is contingent upon another action being done first and the first action is not done on schedule, then the second and any subsequent action will also not get done on schedule.

3. *What resources* will be allocated to each part of the action plan? The resources which must be assigned include the following:

a. Financial resources as specified in the budget or a supplement to the budget for the current year or a commitment to make it a part of the budget for subsequent years affected by the action plan. The amount the strategic plan calls for must equal the amount in the commitment for the current and future budgets of the institution. The president must acknowledge that the cutting back on the expenditure at some future point is an adjustment in the strategic plan. An item in the strategic plan no longer adequately funded is, in effect, removed from the strategic plan. Because so many items in the strategic plan are dependent upon one another, it could mean the failure of strategic planning if the funding now or in the future is not adequately provided.

b. Space resources which are specified in the action plan must be committed to by the institution. It could be the use of specific instructional space at certain times or it could be offices or a part of the grounds. It could mean the building of a new building or an addition to an existing structure. Whatever the space resource which the strategic plan requires must be budgeted and funded in the years indicated in the strategic plan.

The thought might occur to the reader that the strategic plan will preempt the regular budget process. Because the strategic plan involves the leadership of the institution, it involves the same people who are involved in the normal budgeting process. Think of the strategic planning process as budgeting for a multiple-year period in terms of major projects. The annual budgeting process then begins each year with what the commitments are from the strategic planning process rather than the other way around.

c. Other physical resources of the institution might be specified in the strategic plan. Transportation (use of vehicles), use of media (some institutions have their own radio station), use of equipment either away from or at the institution, and related items are included in this category. The strategic plan must not be stymied because an integral item is denied or unavailable due to the lack of commitment of that resource by those who control it.

d. Human resources which are required for implementation of the strategic plan need to be carefully identified with full notation of the nature and timing of these resources in the action plan. This could involve any person within the institution, consultants, board members, or members of some public constituency.

Evaluation and Control

Finally, the personal performance appraisal which must be done on an individual basis uses those individual objectives mentioned above as the basis of appraisal control and reward (Chapter 8). Strategic planning can be successful only if the individuals within the institution accept the responsibility of making the action plans work. The president of the institution is a key figure here, by insisting that personal performance evaluations at all levels and types of positions within the institution are done with a careful review of how well the individuals did in contributing to the success of the strategic plan. This creates a work environment where people know what to do and rewards are tied to performance.

Failure to establish procedures to appraise and control the strategic plan can lead to less than optimal performance. A plan is not complete until the controls are identified and the procedures for recording and transmitting control information to the administrators of the plan are established. Many institutions fail to understand the importance of establishing procedures to appraise and control the planning process. Control should be a natural follow-through in developing the action plan.

Planning and control should be integral processes. The strategic planning process results in a strategic plan. This plan is implemented (activities are performed in the manner described in the action plan) and results are produced. These results might be reflected in services rendered, financial sponsorship, volunteer participation, and image enhancement. Information on these and other Key Result Areas can be used by institutional leaders to compare the results with original objectives to evaluate performances. These performance evaluations identify the areas where decisions must be made to adjust activities, people, or finances.

If a strategic plan does not work out as intended, it could be the result of a number of factors. One possibility is that the institution made a change in direction, a change in plans, after the strategic plan was adopted and before some part of the action plan could be put into effect. It could be because the leadership of the institution, particularly the president, did not continue to make the strategic plan a priority after the planning process was completed but before action plans could be fully implemented. It could be because one or more of the resources listed above were not made available to the extent necessary to ensure success of the strategic plan.

STRATEGIC PLANNING AS AN ONGOING PROCESS

Strategic planning is not simply a singular event to be repeated only every three to five years. The word "process" can be defined as a series of actions or operations conducing to an end. Here we wish to emphasize the ongoing action aspect of the planning process. The actions are the activities in which the institution engages to accomplish objectives and fulfill its mission, and they must continually evolve.

There are several important reasons for viewing strategic planning as a process. First is the idea that a process can be studied and improved. An institution involved in strategic planning will need to review the whole process on an annual basis not only to account for changing external environmental forces and improving internal culture but to improve or refine the plan. Mission statements, vision statements, Key Result Areas, objectives, strategies, action plans, and appraisal techniques can be fine-tuned over time as the planners gain more experience and as new and better information becomes available.

A second reason for viewing strategic planning as a process is that a change in any component of the process will affect most or all of the other components. For example, a change in the mission statement will lead to new analyses, strategies, and evaluations. Thus, major changes which affect the institution must lead to a reevaluation of all the elements of the plan.

Finally, and perhaps most important, is that involvement in the strategic planning process can become the vehicle through which the whole institution mobilizes its energies to accomplish its mission. If all members of the institution can participate in the process in some way, an atmosphere can be created within the institution that implies that doing the right things and doing things right is everybody's job. Participation instills ownership. It's not "my plan" or "their plan," but "our plan" that becomes important; everyone will *want* to make a contribution to make it happen.

STRATEGY IMPLEMENTATION

The focus of this book is on the strategic planning process which results in the development of a strategic plan. This plan becomes the blueprint for carrying out the many activities in which an institution is involved. There are many other issues that determine the effectiveness of an institution that are beyond the scope of this book. These issues essentially revolve around implementing the strategic plan through (1) staffing and training personnel; (2) developing institutional relationships among faculty, staff, and administration; (3) achieving commitment from all persons at all levels; (4) appropriate leadership styles actively in place; and (5) personnel evaluation and reward systems that reward those who help the institution achieve its mission through implementation of the strategic plan.

Our lack of discussion of these topics is due to a desire to keep the length of the book "manageable" for readers and maintain the primary focus on strategic planning for private higher education.

Both effective planning and implementation are needed to create an effective institution. The strategic plan concentrates on "doing the right things" while implementation concentrates on "doing things right." An example of an entire strategic plan for an educational institution is presented in Appendix C.

SUMMARY

This chapter has presented an overview of the strategic planning process in which a series of thought-provoking questions must be answered. The process is a set of integral steps which carry the planners through a sequence that involves providing answers to these questions and then continually rethinking and reevaluating the answers as the institution and its external environment and internal culture change.

A helpful tool to use at this stage is the "Planning Process Worksheet" located at the end of this chapter. This form, when thoughtfully filled out, will provide an assessment of the current position of the institution in terms of its current planning and management. It will help point out where to direct your efforts as you work to improve the efficiency and effectiveness of the institution entrusted to your leadership.

PLANNING PROCESS WORKSHEET

This worksheet is provided to aid your institution in starting the strategic planning process. Use the answers to these questions to provide a foundation for completing the remaining worksheets.

1. Who should be involved in the planning process?

   _____

   _____

   _____

2. Who should provide leadership for the strategic planning meetings?

Outside facilitator/consultant	Administrative leader
In-house facilitator	President
Faculty leader	Other:_____

3. Who will ultimately be responsible for arranging sessions and getting material typed, reproduced, and distributed?

   _____

   _____

   _____

4. Who should be responsible for writing and distributing the report documenting the historical trends/current status of the institution?

   _____

   _____

   _____

5. Who will record action taken and how will this information be disseminated?

    _____

    _____

    _____

6. When (at what stage in the process) and how will the staff, board, membership, or others be involved?

    _____

    _____

    _____

7. Where will planning sessions be held?

    _____

    _____

    _____

8. When will planning sessions be held?

    _____

    _____

    _____

9. What is the timetable for completion of the process?

    _____

    _____

    _____

10. What types of background material do participants need prior to starting the first session?

_____

_____

_____

11. What is the scope of this strategic plan (total institution or department, division, program, etc.)?

_____

_____

_____

12. The time horizon of this strategic plan should be:

    1 to 3 years   5 to 10 years
    3 to 5 years   More than 10 years

13. How will the plan be shared with the larger constituency? What approvals are needed? What protocol needs to be observed?

_____

_____

_____

14. Who will train/supervise staff members in working with their own staff and volunteers in setting objectives, developing action plans, and conducting performance appraisals?

_____

_____

_____

15. How frequently will the process be reviewed and by whom?

_____

_____

_____

16. When should this report, which will include input from all the institution's stakeholders and include planning assumptions, Key Result Areas, and the action plan, be approved and distributed?

_____

_____

_____

Chapter 3

Defining Your Mission and Vision

However brilliant an action might be, it should not be accounted great when it is not the result of a great mission.

— François de La Rochefoucauld

This chapter outlines the first step in the strategic planning process: exploring your vision and defining the mission (purpose). Without a clear and carefully considered mission statement, all other stages of the process will be misguided. Accordingly, we will discuss the development of a vision statement and the value of defining the college or university's mission, describe how to write effective mission statements, and present examples of vision and mission statements.

THE IMPORTANCE OF DEFINING MISSION

Developing the Vision

Probably the most important consideration when developing a strategic plan is to define the mission (purpose) or the "reason for being" for the institution or any specific part of it. As suggested in Chapter 2, a good first step in the process of defining mission is to explore what the institution's vision statement might be. The concept of a vision was introduced in that chapter with the following:

The vision for an institution is a collection of what the institution might be someday if the dreams and aspirations of those in leadership positions were to reach fruition. The vision might include alternative paths the institution might follow and thus not be internally consistent. The vision might include things that few if any of the leaders think will really come to pass in the way in which it is described today. That might be because of changing technology or changing laws that make it difficult, if not impossible, to have a very clear view of what the details in that part of the vision might be.

A vision might be developed through use of the brainstorming technique. A vision can include contributions of what a number of different people think. Some of the ideas produced through such a process might overlap or even conflict. The vision statement will need to deal with issues of conflict but does not have to include hard and fast decisions about these issues. One possibility would be for the vision statement to say that we want to explore A or B and thus include two overlapping or conflicting statements. While internal consistency in a vision statement is nice, that is not a feature of great importance in the vision statement. It becomes very important in the mission statement.

While much has been said in various publications about the need for a mission statement to be very succinct, we believe that the vision statement needs to be as long as necessary to include the various features that the leadership of the institution wishes to include. It should not become a long laundry list, but it could mention a wide range of institutional features in which some major difference from the present is being contemplated.

A vision statement needs to be committed to writing. This makes it more than daydreaming. One reason is to be able to communicate it to others who were not participants in its development. Another is to remind those who did help to develop it as to what was included. A third reason is that the vision statement should be in front of the strategic planning group as the mission statement is being drafted or reviewed. While the mission statement, which reflects what we are attempting to do today, will not likely be entirely consistent with the vision statement, there needs to be coordination. The plans for today need to be going in the same direction as the vision for a future date down the road.

Each institution will need to decide what circulation it wishes to give to its vision statement. Because there are uncertainties in it, it could be misinterpreted, such as by the press. It is not something that the institution wants to be held to as the years unfold. It is suggested that the vision statement not be circulated outside the institution. The mission statement, on the other hand, should be broadly circulated.

One of the most important features of the vision statement is getting people to think about the more distant future in creative ways without the typical restraint about budget, precedent, and acceptance by others. We tend to think of what is practical, and to think in extensions of what we are currently doing. This is true even if we are critical of the current way of doing things. We tend to dismiss that which is very different because we anticipate that anything very different from the present would not be feasible or possible. Thus the session in which the vision statement is prepared needs to have the background setting (perhaps a retreat) in which the leader encourages everyone to think creatively about the ideal, about what might be.

At the end of this chapter, there is a worksheet for the session in which the vision statement is written. The amount of time needed depends upon the size of the group, but probably a half day will be adequate for the task and, in some institutions, much less time might be all that is needed. The recorder for the group needs to be carefully chosen so that ideas which will come only once are captured at the time they are said. The person must be able to catch very broad concepts very quickly and have the facility to write down a complex idea succinctly.

The Mission Statement

Writing an initial mission statement is usually a difficult process. Drucker (1974) notes the importance of identifying an institution's mission by emphasizing that it is the process of organizing to satisfy a need in the marketplace. The mission concept should be student-oriented (client being served) in that it is defined by the desire the customer satisfies when a product or a service is purchased. In higher education terms, the student must be satisfied with the education he or she receives at the time that the education is received. Thus, satisfying the student (customer or client) is the mission of every institution.

Institutions need a clear definition of mission (purpose) because that is the only way to obtain clear and realistic objectives for the future. It is the foundation for Key Result Areas, objectives, strategies, and action plans. The mission is the starting point for the design of managerial structure and jobs (Drucker, 1974) as well as every other institutional feature. Clearly, if mission is defined casually or introspectively, the basis for how an institution goes about achieving its objectives rests on shaky foundations. If we are not clear in what we are about, then almost anything we do, regardless of its true effectiveness, can be made to sound like it was the best course of action. This can be self-deluding and self-defeating, taking us away from the long-run basis for our existence: meeting student needs. As Calvin Coolidge put it, "No enterprise can exist for itself alone. It ministers to some great need, it performs some great service not for itself but for others; or failing therein it ceases to be profitable and ceases to exist."

It is not easy to formulate a mission statement. The mission statement should reflect at least a portion of the vision statement of what the institution wants to be. Members should try to visualize what they want the institution to be and then set out to write this as a mission statement which can be agreed upon. If they can see where they are going and have an image of the real mission of the institution, the implementation of their plans will fall more easily into place.

It is important to understand this concept of vision in order to be a successful institution. The mission is what unites the faculty, administration, and staff and spurs them to higher performance. Without a long-term perspective, an institution will continually swerve off course instead of moving with steadiness and certainty toward its goals.

This mission statement sets the stage for all planning. A clear mission statement provides a starting point for determining objectives as specific measures of mission effectiveness. Objectives, which are covered later in the text, must by their very nature contribute to achieving what is in the mission statement. Without objectives and then an action plan for their implementation, a mission statement becomes an empty platitude.

Private Christian colleges were the subject of a study looking for the best managed colleges of this type (Oosting, 1996). In this study it was discovered that of the ten colleges studied in depth, the mission statement was central in each of these institutions in guiding the short-term as well as the long-term activities of the institution.

In summary, six reasons might be suggested for an institution to have a mission statement:

1. It provides a reason for being, an explanation to those in the institution as well as those outside it as to why the institution exists.
2. It sets boundaries around the operations and thus defines what will be done and what will not be done.
3. It describes the need the institution is attempting to meet in the world and how it is going to respond to that need.
4. It acts as the foundation on which the primary objectives of the institution can be based.
5. It helps to form the basis for the internal culture of the institution.
6. It helps to communicate to those both inside and outside the institution as to what it is all about.

BASIC ELEMENTS IN A MISSION STATEMENT

In developing a mission statement, several basic elements should be reflected:

1. *History.* Every college or university has a history which includes past problems, accomplishments, objectives, and policies. The mission statement should reflect the historical significance of such characteristics.
2. *Distinctive competencies.* This element reflects what the institution is uniquely equipped to do because of its location, personnel, resources, or historical position. While most institutions can do many things, they can do some things so well that they have an advantage over other institutions in those areas.
3. *Needs, segments, and technology.* The mission statement must reflect what will be done (needs met or values received by

students), whom it will be done for (student groups or segments to be served since we can't be all things to all people), and what technology will be used (how needs will be met).

4. *External Environment/Internal Culture.* Each college or university operates in an external environment and an internal culture that dictate the opportunities and threats which must be dealt with when a mission statement is developed. Laws structuring insurance policies and fear of disease transmission are examples of external environmental factors which influence an institution's ability to achieve its mission. Examples of the internal culture are how people relate to one another, the significance placed upon certain events, and levels of quality.

5. *Leadership.* Is the mission statement a passing group of words that simply describe an institution or is it a manifesto that the institution wishes to proactively pursue? The difference is in the leadership of the institution. The extent to which the institution has leadership, beginning with the president, the greater is the likelihood that the institution will be one of those which attains much of its mission statement.

It is not unusual for an institution to work on a mission statement for months or even years before deciding that it really reflects what the institution wants to become. Once developed, the mission statement should not be a once-and-forever document. As the college or university adapts itself to the demands of a changing environment, so should the mission statement reflect this adaptation. It must be reviewed periodically and updated as appropriate to continually reflect the institution's fundamental purposes. However, the mission statement should be a stable document, not subject to whims and day-to-day changes. The institution must emphasize stability in the basics as a value.

Developing a mission statement is a difficult and thought-provoking process when approached correctly, but it must be done. As stated earlier, what an institution does (objectives and strategies) should flow from what the institution is (mission or purpose).

WRITING A MISSION STATEMENT

The following list provides helpful tips for writing and evaluating a mission statement:

1. Determine your fundamental reason for being. Part of this is evident from the institution's history. For an institution under development, this means expressly determining what need satisfaction you will offer your client, the student. If the institution is currently operating and not a new start-up, this means moving its thinking beyond simply what it now does. You must specifically identify what the need satisfaction *should* be for your institution. Identifying your basic mission for existence also means wrestling with what need satisfaction your institution might be offering in the future.

    One outcome of these considerations should be a section of the statement that is specific enough to offer guidance to the institution's stakeholders in the near term. But there should also be a general aspect that looks to the future and provides "wiggle room" for your institution to adapt and grow with future needs. Done effectively, these aspects of the mission statement serve as a touchstone, reminding the institution's stakeholders why they do what they do.

2. What are the distinctive competencies of the institution? How should they be reflected in the mission statement? The mission statement should reflect these competencies. The mission statement should be specific enough to set the institution apart from others, yet not restrict the institution unnecessarily from accomplishing its purpose.

3. Determine the scope of the mission. This involves determining who the institution intends to serve. Proper deliberation here focuses attention outside the nuts and bolts of internal activities. It forces consideration of the intended recipients of the institution's services. At a practical level, scope identifies the breadth of delivery—local neighborhood, community-wide, regional, national, or international. If the operation is part of a larger institution, the parent institution becomes part of the clientele served since the mission should support the parent institution's mission on the one hand, and be accountable to it

on the other. In effect, writing a mission statement for a unit such as a college within a university or an academic department means delivering part of the larger institution's mission. For instance, some colleges and universities have a mission that seeks to serve an entire nation. But such an institution should define its mission in terms of applying the national mission to a specific constituency such as the local community in which it is located.

4. What are the needs, segments, and technology affecting the institution? How do they impact the mission statement of the institution? Is the institution self-supporting or does it require much from its constituencies in order to survive or prosper? How does technology affect the mission of the institution?

5. Identify your principal methods for delivering need satisfaction. This issue focuses on the basic activities and functions your college or university will employ to meet the needs of your student clientele. Verbs are the key here. "Teach" or "do research" and "perform community service" are all action words representative of basic delivery activities. Here, the institution must deal with the issue of to what extent it will be overt in reaching out to the community where the college is located by offering what that constituency needs and wants in other locations and through other than traditional delivery systems, as opposed to offering only what professors or current students wish to see the institution offer and doing so only in traditional delivery systems.

6. Study the external environment and the internal culture to determine how each should impact the mission statement.

7. When unit planning is involved, determine that portion of the larger institution's mission statement for which the unit doing the planning is accountable. While the college's national mission might include many services such as national recruiting, alumni services, job placement, and research services, a college's chemistry department capabilities might be more limited, excluding, for instance, any offerings off campus. The mission statement should reflect these differences where they exist.

8. Prepare a rough draft of the mission statement that covers the mission of the group and the major activities it performs (or

begin with the existing statement). With a working team, such as the administrative staff and board of trustees or the planning team, a rough draft mission statement can be developed at an all-day meeting using an outside facilitator who is familiar with communications techniques, group processes, and the concept of mission statements. The meeting could begin with each individual writing a personal version of the mission statement. When these drafts are all assembled, the group can review each one for clarity and understanding. Finally, those portions that are similar can be condensed so that only areas of wide disagreement are left. At this point, negotiations can be carried out between members of the group until there is general agreement on all points ("I am able to live with this"). The final result is the rough draft of the mission statement. If there already is a mission statement in existence that the planning group wishes to begin with, it can be examined phrase by phrase to determine meaning and the degree to which the group can subscribe to the agreed upon meaning.

To review, a mission statement needs to be built around several points:

1. Internal operations and functions—typically this includes a description of the fundamental activities the institution engages in, specifically, the basic services provided such as education, training, counseling, feeding, housing, and so on. This aspect of the statement thus answers the "what do we do?" question.
2. External clientele—this part of the statement focuses on identifying the customers to be served by the institution. This might include descriptions of demographic characteristics as well as geographic boundaries (such as the Boston, Massachusetts Standard Metropolitan Area [SMA]). This portion of the statement emphasizes answers to the "who do we serve?" question.
3. Needs served—the emphasis here is on the needs of constituencies that will be met. These are the ultimate ends we hope to achieve such as better health, more productive citizenry, a greater appreciation of the arts, and so on. Philosophically, this section identifies who we are and hope to be, giving our mem-

bership an identity to hold onto in uncertain times and the leeway to stretch toward new services and greater goal attainment of existing ones.

SAMPLE MISSION STATEMENTS

It might be helpful at this point to examine some mission statements prepared by various institutions. Note that these statements reflect the uniqueness of the institutions in terms of their reasons for being and also serve as guidelines for what the institutions should be doing. These statements were developed through a process involving many people. Initial statements were revised many times to add specificity and clarity to the terms used to define mission.

Biola University, La Mirada, California

The mission of Biola University is to be a Christian university providing education at the baccalaureate and post-baccalaureate levels in biblical studies and theology, in the liberal arts and sciences, and in selected applied and professional fields. It is to be Christian in the sense that the biblical Christian world view serves as the all-encompassing framework and integrating basis for the entire content and conduct of the institution. It is to be a university in the full traditional meaning of the term; with knowledge and understanding being generated and disseminated, with students and faculty continually developing to high levels their cognitive and effective potential; and with society being served beneficially thereby. In combining the two terms, Christian and university, considerable emphasis is placed upon the scholarly integration of biblical faith with all of the fields of learning, and also upon the practical interrelationships and interdependencies of faith, learning and living as they are developed throughout the curriculum and the lifestyle.

The mission of the University is to produce graduates who are (a) competent in their fields of study, (b) knowledgeable in biblical studies, and (c) earnest Christians equipped to serve the Christian community and society at large.

There are two additional "products" of the University, both of which are to be viewed as outgrowths of the task of producing graduates of its baccalaureate and post-baccalaureate programs and not separate from it. One consists of the scholarly contributions to knowledge and understanding which are generated by students and faculty in the disciplines and in integration with the biblical Christian world view. The other consists of public services as students, faculty and staff make their professional and personal expertise available to the Christian community and to society at large throughout the world.

College of St. Joseph, Rutland, Vermont

The College of St. Joseph is a small, private college that educates men and women for lives of continuing personal growth, intellectual development and community service. Its educational programs are implemented within the context of Christian values and Roman Catholic traditions.

The College also serves as an educational cultural resource in its immediate environment, using assessment of community needs as a guide to program development. To fulfill this mission, the College:

1. Offers curricula that emphasize preparation for careers of vital importance to the surrounding community. These career-oriented programs include both theoretical and practical training and are built upon a liberal studies foundation.
2. Maintains a supportive living and learning environment for students of varying ages and abilities.
3. Involves its internal and external constituencies in the identification of educational needs.
4. Promotes flexibility, innovation and individualization in responding to student and community needs.

Fisk University, Nashville, Tennessee

Fisk's mission today, as described officially by the Board of Trustees in a statement most recently revised in 1986, remains that of an institution committed first to teaching of the liberal arts, and to the preparation of leaders. Fisk is also, however, committed to involving both its faculty and its most advanced students in original research—since the passing on of the liberal arts tradition is not merely the transmission of dead or static knowledge; rather, the liberal arts tradition involves the recognition that knowledge is continually developing. The University aims, in short, "to provide liberal education of the highest quality. The ultimate goal," according to the Trustees' 1986 statement, "is to prepare students to be skilled, resourceful, and imaginative leaders who will address effectively the challenges of life in a technological society, a pluralistic nation, and a multicultural world."

Goshen College, Goshen, Indiana

Goshen College is a four-year liberal arts college dedicated to the development of informed, sensitive, responsible Christians. As a ministry of the Mennonite Church, we seek to integrate Christian values with educational and professional life. As a community of faith and learning, we strive to foster personal, intellectual, spiritual and social growth. We view education as a moral activity that produces servant-leaders of the church and the world.

Hood College, Frederick, Maryland

At the heart of the Hood College mission is a century-long commitment to the education and advancement of women to their preparation for purposeful lives and careers. Continuing this 100-year tradition of excellence, Hood College enters its second century preparing all students to meet the challenges of the future. Maintaining its special commitment to providing a residential experience for undergraduate women, as well as to providing graduate and undergraduate education for both women and men, the Hood community is enriched as it responds to the diverse intellectual, professional, and personal goals of individual students of all races, ethnicities, and ages. The Hood environment, both in and out of the classroom, promotes the understanding that learning is interactive, between individuals and disciplines; that the exchange of ideas must involve the exploration of values; and that education requires lifelong engagement. The Hood College community at all levels aspires to the highest standards of academic achievement and reaffirms the College's commitment to preparing students for the personal, societal, and global challenges of the future.

Malone College, Canton, Ohio

The purpose of Malone is to provide students with an educational experience based on Biblical faith. This experience will prepare them to make informed moral and ethical choices, equip them to cope with a pluralistic society, and enable them to serve the church, community and world. This is implemented by:

- Facilitation of a life-long process of intellectual and spiritual growth;
- Discovery of knowledge through interaction with all disciplines of learning (Scripture, arts, sciences and humanities);
- Exposure to significant ideas in an environment of investigation and evaluation;
- Involvement in the life and institutions of urban society;
- Development of an international perspective through cross-cultural experiences;
- Preparation for a creative and productive career;
- Providing opportunities to understand and accept a personal faith with Jesus Christ.

Northwest College, Kirkland, Washington

The purpose of Northwest College is to provide, in an evangelical Christian context, higher education which will:

1. Develop the whole person through general studies integrated with biblical knowledge;
2. Include professional and vocational skills in the student's preparation for service in the world;
3. Help to fulfill the Great Commission and to propagate the historic faith of the sponsoring church.

Nyack College, Nyack, New York

Endeavoring to reflect the values of the Kingdom of God, Nyack College, as an agency of The Christian and Missionary Alliance, seeks to assist students in their spiritual, intellectual, professional, and social growth while preparing them for effective service to Christ and His church.

Providence College, Winnipeg, Manitoba, Canada

The Mission of Providence College is to educate students at a university level to think, live, and serve effectively as Christians in the church and in society.

Rocky Mountain College, Billings, Montana

Rocky Mountain College is a community of learners working together to better understand who we are and how to live. As a liberal arts college, our responsibility is to educate ourselves and the ever-changing larger community, recognizing the importance of the liberal arts as the foundation of all learning for academic, professional, and life-long development.

As a college founded in the Christian tradition, we seek to understand that tradition in an open and non-sectarian way, upholding the importance of one's own beliefs with respect for and fair consideration of others' beliefs. As a college in the Mountain West, we seek to understand the history and environment of our region as a bridge to understanding the history and environment of the larger world.

We value the diversity and the interrelatedness of knowledge, the importance of rational inquiry and open discussion, and the interdependence of all life.

We believe individual success is characterized not only by independent and creative thought, but also by evidence of an ethical commitment to others. Rocky Mountain College seeks to prepare students to act responsibly as members of an academically, socially, ecologically, and spiritually interconnected world.

Town and Country School, Tulsa, Oklahoma

Town and Country offers a second chance for success to Learning Disabled and Attention Deficit Disordered (with or without hyperactivity) children who have not succeeded in other public or private school special education programs. The mission of our school is to help each child compensate for his or her specific learning disabilities, increase the child's self-esteem, self-confidence, and social skills, and return the child to a traditional school classroom as quickly as possible, prepared to achieve his or her full potential. We strive to constantly provide the highest quality individualized educational services in the state for these special children, who are in pre-school (four years of age) through eighth grade.

The mission of the School is to create a stronger community by helping children with special educational needs not only overcome their disabilities, but develop the critical thinking and life skills necessary to their becoming responsible, productive adults.

EVALUATING A MISSION STATEMENT

The list below can be used as a guide to evaluate a mission statement. The idea is to come up with a statement that really represents what the institution wants to be or should be to survive.

1. Broadness and continuity of application. The statement should be broad enough to cover all significant areas of activity expected of the institution without a specific termination period indicated.
2. Functional commitment. The nature of the works, tasks, or activities to be performed must be defined in terms that will determine clearly the validity of the group or institution.
3. Resource commitment. The statement should include a commitment to cost-effective utilization of available resources.
4. Unique or distinctive nature of work. Every unit in an institution should make some unique or distinctive contribution. If there are two or more units in an institution with identical mission statements, the risk of duplicated effort is obvious.
5. Description of academic and other services to be offered.
6. Description of group or groups to be served.
7. Geographical area to be served.

Sometimes it is useful to use a series of questions to evaluate a mission statement after it is written. A "no" answer to one of the questions means the statement needs to be reworded to more clearly reflect the institution's basic reason for being. The following list of questions might be useful to you:

1. Does it contain all important commitments?
2. Does it clearly state the function?
3. Is there a clear determination of relationships to any parent institution (such as department to a college or a college to a university)?
4. Is it distinct from the mission statements of other groups in the institution or other institutions?
5. Is it short, to the point, and understandable?
6. Is it continuing in nature?
7. Does it state to whom the group is accountable?

While the word "service" is often included in the mission statement of many institutions, fundamentally the mission statement needs to answer specifically the question of why the institution is needed in the first place. Plenty of other institutions exist. Discuss and know clearly what needs you are meeting and for whom. In answering the "for whom" question, a mission statement can reflect whether the institution wants to be local, regional, national, or international.

SUMMARY

Hopefully, you have caught the significance of verbalizing and putting in writing the vision statement and the mission statement adopted by the department, college, or university. By committing it to writing, the institution has, in effect, expressly stated the unique reason for the institution's existence. This provides the sense of identity, direction, and focus for what the institution does. What an institution does must be a function of its mission. The mission statement translates the long-run dreams and aspirations in the vision statement into tangible form and builds a strong foundation for its fulfillment.

MISSION STATEMENT WORKSHEET

This worksheet will aid you in writing a mission statement for your institution.

1. Write a statement for the following areas:

    Internal operations statement:

    _____

    _____

    _____

    External clientele (environment) statement:

    _____

    _____

    _____

    Describe the internal culture of the institution:

    _____

    _____

    _____

    What needs are served by the institution?

    _____

    _____

    _____

2. Without attempting to write a vision statement at this point, record here some of the items that might appear in a vision statement (see discussion in Chapter 3 for the difference between a vision statement and a mission statement).

    _____

    _____

    _____

3. Now prepare a first draft mission statement:

_____

_____

_____

4. Now evaluate the statement:

    a. Does it define boundaries within which your institution will operate?

    _____

    _____

    _____

    b. Does it define the need(s) that your institution is attempting to meet?

    _____

    _____

    _____

    c. Does the institution have a local, regional, national, or international scope?

    _____

    _____

    _____

    d. Does it define the market (students) that your institution is reaching?

    _____

    _____

    _____

e. Does it include the word "service," or a word with similar meaning?

_____

_____

_____

5. Has there been input from appropriate institutional members?

_____

_____

_____

6. Next, submit it to others familiar with the institution to evaluate your mission statement and offer suggestions on improving the statement. In order words, does the statement say to others what you want it to say?

_____

_____

_____

Chapter 4

Determining the Internal Culture: "Core Values and Philosophy"

WHAT DO WE MEAN BY INTERNAL CULTURE?

The term "culture" is typically used in the context of a large group of people such as an ethnic group. The culture of an ethnic group or a nation is always distinct from that of other ethnic groups and nations. As sociologists analyze that culture, they come to understand the people in the culture including their beliefs, values, customs, traditions, economy, and other distinguishing features. The culture is not something we analyze or judge as being either good or bad (although there might be some aspects of a culture we approve or disapprove of depending upon how it relates to our values and beliefs). An ethnic or national culture describes a people. It tells us how they are distinctive including how they set priorities. Usually there are some lessons to be learned from studying a culture other than our own.

How do these ethnic or national cultures come to be what they are at the time they are studied? They come about in small, incremental segments which are often not noticed as they enter the culture. All cultures continually change, but they change in ways that are often imperceptible by those who either live in the culture or are living in other cultures in the same time frame. Some change is purposeful; that is, it is brought about on purpose. This is usually from people within that culture.

Much of the change comes about, however, by discoveries, emphasis upon history, perceptions of reality (with varying degrees of distortion), and goals of a people. They are affected by weather and by technology. The culture of a people is always complex and seldom understood very fully even by those who live within that culture. Much the same kind of process occurs within human institutions. Each human organization, even an organization with only a single individual within it, has a distinctive organizational culture (sometimes called corporate culture). Organizational culture is made up of the composite of the personalities of the individuals in the organization past and present, plus the physical environment, and a host of related factors such as the type of work being done, weather, external pressures from government, competition, and public reaction/support, as well as attitudes currently being expressed within the organization (enthusiasm, apathy, or disdain). All of this comes together to form a distinct scenario for each organization.

This scenario or culture determines the output of the organization more than any other factor including education and skill of the people working in the organization. It is because of this factor that organizational culture must be considered in any effort toward strategic planning. Strategic planning for a particular organizational culture is possible only if the future direction is either consistent with that culture and the direction it is heading, or the culture feels such a pressure on its possible continuation that it is willing to break with its past in order to have a future at all. Some organizations, of course, would rather perish than to change to something inconsistent with the values in that organizational culture.

International business, cross-national trade, travel, in fact, everything international is affected by national or ethnic cultures. Colleges, universities, seminaries, and every other part of private higher education is deeply affected by the internal (organizational) culture of the institutions that make up private higher education. There is no choice. It is simply a fact. To lead, to plan in private higher education requires an understanding of the concept of organizational culture (or as we are more likely to say in higher education, institutional culture), a knowledge of what it is in the organizations where any of us attempt to serve, and the ability to affect that culture in positive ways.

DEVELOPMENT OF THE CONCEPT OF ORGANIZATIONAL CULTURE

The study of what we now call "organizational culture" or "corporate culture" dates back to Henry Murray and his associates at the Harvard Psychological Clinic in 1938 (Oosting, 1968). Their work had the purpose of studying personality. To accomplish this, Murray began to study the effects of the immediate environment on the individual. This emphasis upon the individual is based upon the assumption that the culture formed by other personalities in the same workplace will have a major impact upon individual personality development. In effect, the study of individual personalities led to the study of the personalities of organizations. This organizational personality, the organizational environment, came to be called "corporate culture." The concept, however, extends to all organizations regardless of size.

It is interesting that subsequent observation of the relationship between the personality of an institution and the personality of its leadership leads us to conclude that the personality of an institution often tends to take on the personality of its president. Many small colleges in the early 1900s that were led for decades by the same president were examples of this (such as Johnson Bible College near Knoxville, Tennessee). At the same time, readers might be able to recall a situation, probably more recently, in which a relatively long tenure as president had no direct relationship to dynamic leadership of the institution. The latter institution probably lacked focus and probably did little strategic planning.

The study of organizational culture blossomed during the 1970s and 1980s and is now considered a major factor in what makes the difference between and among organizations. It is in this context that we consider organizational culture in our study of organizational planning in private higher education. The organizational culture tends to define what is possible, what is feasible, in the future of an organization. This is because the organizational culture reflects the prevailing thinking within the organization.

The future of an organization is confined by what that organization thinks is possible in its future and what that thinking leads those in the organization to conclude as to what they want in their organizational future. What we think is possible and what we want to happen will set the outer boundaries (parameters) of what is possible in our future. An example of what is possible occurred at King College in Bristol, Tennessee, which went through a deliberate, major change in its culture in 1980 when impending closure brought an influx of major donors who, in turn, brought about a different emphasis for the institution and thus a different culture.

"Organizational culture" and "corporate culture" are the terms most often used in the study of internal culture, but because higher education tends to think of itself as a group of institutions rather than organizations, we will use the term "institutional culture" in the rest of this book.

WHAT ARE THE "CORE VALUES" AND "PHILOSOPHY" ON A CAMPUS?

It is important to make the effort to determine what people in an institution think is possible and what they would like to see happen. This thinking represents the "core values" in the institution. In the case of a college or university, it represents those values that guide the learning process and the level and type of support given to the learning process by the rest of the institution. The "philosophy" on campus is another way of expressing what "core values" are held by those who are in a position to control or affect the thinking on a campus (use of both formal and informal authority).

While those of us in the academic world would tend to reject the idea that thinking is controlled or strongly affected on a campus, it is clear that in colleges and universities, like all other organizations, the institutional culture will permit certain things to be said and done, will encourage other statements, and will prohibit or put penalties upon other thoughts and behaviors. Academic cultures tend to be slightly more open to a range of thinking but will still clearly place limits on what is acceptable and what is encouraged. For example, while the thinking in for-profit corporations often reflects rather conservative values, the larger college and university campuses will typically place a higher value on liberal views which emphasize the rights of the individual over the rights of society (less likely in a small, Christian college). Expressing a liberal view in a corporate setting is likely to be as popular as a clearly conservative view on a campus. This is a reflection of the cultures on that campus and in that corporation. However, these same campuses are typically very fiscally conservative and not tolerant of views advocating higher education reform.

It is essential to know these "core values" when attempting to plan in any institutional culture. The future can never be something which the culture in that institution will not tolerate. Thus, a planner must "know the territory" in order to be successful. While planning is not simply a straight line projection from the past through the present to the future, there are few right turns and left turns. Learning the past and the present of an institution is essential to the planning process, for it will give definition to what is possible and to what is likely to be acceptable in the future.

THE RELATIONSHIP BETWEEN CULTURE AND VISION/MISSION

While the vision of an institution is a statement of what people within it see as a desirable dream for where the institution might be someday, and mission is where the institution is attempting to go today, the institutional culture is a statement of what the institution actually is in its daily thoughts and behaviors. Institutional culture thus can be the inhibitor or the encourager of an institution toward achieving its stated mission. To state it another way, institutional culture will determine whether a particular mission can be attained.

As a result, the development of a mission statement that the institutional culture will not allow is both foolish and a waste of time. Leadership in affecting that culture must come first if a segment of the proposed mission statement is a higher priority than maintaining the aspect of the institutional culture which conflicts with it. Then, if the change in the institutional culture is leaning in the same direction as the proposed mission statement, that mission statement moves closer to describing the actual situation. The process of drafting or reviewing a mission statement or a vision statement requires a knowledge of the prevailing culture at the institution at that time.

HOW CAN INSTITUTIONAL CULTURE BE MEASURED?

If it is important to know the existing institutional culture (know the past and the present of the institution), the logical question then becomes, how do you become aware of the prevailing institutional culture? Is it something which can be measured, which can be described?

There are two possible approaches to measuring institutional culture. One is to study certain aspects of that culture such as personality, existence of conflict, openness to change, or willingness to follow leadership. There are instruments which could help an institution to measure these aspects of the culture.

The *Thomas-Kilmann Conflict Mode Instrument* (Thomas and Kilmann, 1974), for example, will help an institution to see how it defines, uses, and resolves conflict. Elias Porter (1989) has developed the *Strength Deployment Inventory* which can assist in understanding the institutional strengths held by the individual members of a particular culture.

The *Learning Style Inventory* (Kolb, 1985) can help an institution to determine how people in that institution learn and how they will perceive the possibilities for the future. For example, the instrument will identify those in the institution who are the "divergers"–those who are the most likely to have an active imagination and have the ability to recognize problems.

Another possibility is the simulation exercise like *Star Power* (1969) by R. Garry Shirts. Used in a group, this will help people to understand the effectiveness of individuals vs. groups in solving problems. While chapters one and two address the role of the individual vs. groups in the planning process, this type of exercise can help an institution to see whether it is composed primarily of "Lone Rangers" or if the prevailing culture is team work.

The other approach is to study the complete culture of an institution. While the study of institutional culture started with Murray in the 1930s, instruments have not become widely used in either the corporate or higher education scenes. The reader is referred to *Organizational Climate and Culture*, edited by Benjamin Schneider (1990), where in chapters five and six the issue of research in institutional culture is treated. Other insights can be found in *Gaining Control of the Corporate Culture*, in which the editors, Ralph H. Kilmann and others (1985), provide some of the best of the current thinking about how to approach corporate culture.

Edgar Schein in *Organizational Culture and Leadership* (1985) provides possibly the best understanding of the concept of institutional culture and how a college or university might go about measuring the culture it has. Schein ties the ability to affect the culture of an institution to the ability to effectively demonstrate leadership in that institution. Thus, Schein emphasizes the ability to not only understand culture, but also to be able to affect it, to change it.

An instrument specifically designed to measure the culture in the small private college is *The College Culture Inventory* (1985) by Kenneth W. Oosting and R. Bertram Allen. This instrument has segments to be administered to students, faculty, administrators, and board members leading to the analysis of dimensions of culture within that institution. Once these dimensions have been determined, the possibilities for planning in that college or university can be more clearly seen.

The instruments mentioned here suggest that it is possible to learn about the culture within which people work and plan. Further, the viewpoint of the writers is that taking the time and expending the effort to learn about the culture in which planning is taking place is essential to the planning process. You must have an understanding of the current culture within an institution in order to have any understanding of what future is either possible or desirable for that institution.

What Will Such Information Tell Us?

Culture measurement is not yet to the level that it can place all institutions into types and thus tell its planners that it must start with a particular set of planning assumptions. Just as no two individuals are the same, no two institutions are the same. This makes the measure of the culture more interesting (there are lots of possible outcomes) and productive (it tells us who we are today so that we can use this information in planning our future).

The important part of the question of what will such information tell us relates to how information about the culture of an institution can help us to plan in that institution.

Information about the culture within an institution will provide us with information about aspects of the institution which are essential to the planning process. Some of them are:

1. Attitudes and perspectives about planning,
2. The informal structure of the institution,
3. The appropriateness of staffing decisions past and present,
4. Perceptions about institutional leadership,
5. What management policies are supported within the culture,
6. What management and personal practices are supported and which are frowned upon or punished by the institution,
7. The preferred leadership style (the one likely to be successful),
8. Peculiarities relating to institutions of that type,
9. The importance of controls within the institution, and
10. The role of evaluation within the institution.

These are just a few of the areas in which knowing more about the culture could be helpful in the planning process. In the specific situation governing a specific institution, planners should be able to identify a significant number of others.

How Does It Help in Planning?

Knowledge about the organizational or institutional culture enables those involved in planning to plan from more of a knowledge base than is true in institutions where the culture is known only partially and then by word of mouth. Knowing about the institution allows the planners to know about what is likely to succeed in the future for that institution and what directions are not likely to succeed. For example, an institution with a low tolerance for change (a feature of its culture) is not likely to be open to a new program or a new way of doing things in a major office. Knowledge of the institution's past and present will certainly be helpful in shaping its future.

Is There an Ideal Institutional Culture?

An institution can work toward the culture that reflects the values held within that institution. While some values, such as academic integrity, are common to all institutions, some values will overlap between institutions. However, institutions not only do not share some values, they also give different priorities to commonly held values. Thus, for a campus to have an organizational (institutional) culture like some other institution is possible but not likely because the two institutions do not have the same history and do not share the identical values and priorities. Ideal is defined in different ways by different people and groups. What is ideal for one institution could be unacceptable to some others.

Institutions can be ideal for the set of values they hold as an academic community. This assumes that the institution is conscious of any shared values which might be held within the institution. This should not be assumed as a given, however. In fact, it is suggested here that few institutions have a very clear notion about the values and priorities they hold. The institutions most likely to have a good picture of their values and priorities are those which take pride in being different from other institutions in their purpose, such as single niche colleges and seminaries. Other specialized graduate schools or undergraduate schools such as Bible colleges are cognizant of their uniqueness. The institution which sees itself as modeling its programs and goals to be like other institutions with higher prestige is the least likely to really understand what its values and priorities are because they are defined by others and viewed not in the abstract but in practice. When an institution models the practices of another institution, it cannot be assumed that it understands the rationale or theory behind those practices.

It is suggested here that every institution needs to become very aware of its values and how it wishes to prioritize them. The institution most likely to cease to exist is the one which has only a vague and copied notion of its reason for existence. Institutions, like people, must know where they are trying to go in order to have any chance of success in getting there.

VALUES AND PRIORITIES

It might be legitimately asked, "What are the values and priorities of a given institution?" The quick way of determining this is to look in three places. First is the institution's budget and audit, second is in how it spends its time, and third is in what it talks about. Let's look at each of the three.

Budget and Audit

First, how does budget and audit relate to values and priorities? A budget is a plan for how to allocate the financial resources of the institution. It is usually an annual plan from July 1 through June 30. Finances are translated into programs, people, and processes. Money is attached, in varying amounts, to the priorities of the institution. The budget is the plan. The audit says how well the institution followed the plan. As mentioned in an earlier chapter, the strategic plan carries within the budget implications for a multiyear period while the annual budget must begin with those commitments and bring detail to the budget for that fiscal year.

Every institution has limited financial resources. The budget is the planning document for the manner in which those limited resources are allocated throughout the institution. While there are probably not significant differences between institutions of similar size, purpose, and scope, there are still differences which reveal much about the values and priorities of the institution. A budget which includes faculty development says there is a value placed upon developing faculty to their potential. A budget which has a very limited allocation for the library is saying that this learning resource is either already a great collection, there is very good outside funding, or that the library is not very important.

Even institutions which claim to not do any planning have a budget and an audit. In fact, they do plan. Unfortunately, many institutional budgets are put together by a small number of people in that college or university. As a result, there is little awareness or ownership of the budget priorities stated. This leads to many requests to spend in ways not covered by the budget. When this happens, the audit will reflect a different set of priorities from the budget.

There could be an additional problem created by the auditors when they fail to use the same categories as used in the budget. When they do this, it means that there is no direct comparison between the two documents. The audit then tells the institution only whether it has met its budget plan in very global terms such as total income and total cost. Presidents should never allow auditors to use categories other than the ones used by the institution in its budget. Likewise, if the audit includes some categories required by, for example, the U.S. government or standard accounting practice, the budget should be adjusted to reflect these categories as well.

Allocation of Time

The second view of the values and priorities of the institution is in how it spends its time. What is the annual calendar of the institution? Colleges and universities over the past quarter-century have been moving toward shorter semesters and thus a shorter academic year. What happens at the institution the rest of the calendar year? Anything? Does the institution go on a "summer schedule" of shorter hours for the offices due to less work to be done, and does the faculty depart to take a second job or read or travel?

There are 365 days in a calendar year. It is up to the institution to determine how that time resource will be utilized. Elementary, secondary, and collegiate institutions are already recognized in our culture as being the most wasteful of the calendar year. What are institutions doing about this? Most are doing very little but this is changing as year-round programs appear on campuses. In the planning process, the institution has the opportunity to look at this resource.

The Topic of Conversation

The third indicator of institutional values is in what the people in the institution talk about when they are together and when they communicate with others outside the institution. Is the rhetoric the same as it was 25 or 50 years ago but with different examples? Or does discussion focus upon core values of the institution and current ways of instilling them further within the institution? Does discussion in the faculty break area focus upon football or the weather? Are there faculty seminars in which significant ideas are discussed? Are faculty members and all other staff encouraged to come up with new ideas, new ways of doing things? The institutional culture will either encourage or discourage certain topics to be openly discussed. The writers have done work on campuses throughout the United States and Canada and have observed a very different set of discussion topics from one institution to another. However, most institutions hover around topics similar from one campus to another. Look at your own campus to determine what is on the minds of people there. This will reveal something about what is important on your campus.

HOW CAN YOU PLAN A CULTURE?

You don't plan a culture. You plan to develop certain values. Values which permeate what the institution does, what it says, how it allocates its budget, how it spends its time, and what it talks about are the overarching values which determine the culture of that campus. What are the values on the campuses with which you are the most familiar?

The writers are not suggesting a particular set of values for an institution. These values need to flow from the mission statement and should be unique to each institution. It is essential in the planning process that the institution determine what those values currently are.

Values of an institution can change. However, unless the institution is under heavy duress, such as the threat of impending closure, values will not change very quickly. A new president, a new campus, a new mission statement (all if considerably different from the previous one) could have the impact of bringing major changes in values. Without those major events, however, values, and thus the culture, will change only slowly.

CULTURE AND LEADERSHIP

Edgar Schein (1985) in his book, *Organizational Culture and Leadership*, discusses the relationship between culture and leadership. His bottom line point is that if a leader cannot change the culture, he or she cannot provide leadership. It is only through impacting the culture that leadership really takes place. Being president or dean or chair without being able to change the culture is merely presiding over an existing culture. At the end of such a tenure, the culture might have entered into change due to external factors or the leadership of others, but not because of the presiding over the existing culture.

Let's assume that you want to provide leadership in a college, university, graduate school, or seminary (or some segment of one). Where do you start? It is suggested here that you start by examining the values which provide the underpinning for the institution. Some of these values will be very apparent. Is the football stadium or the library the center of the campus? Is student learning central to institutional values and priorities? Look at the items above that suggest much about an institution: budget, time, and topics. Some values will be difficult to determine. These are likely to be among the most significant. That is, they might do more to determine the campus culture than those which are very apparent. They might be in such things as the regard for the individual, the importance of ethical practice, or the likelihood of people saying what they mean to say as opposed to having to read between the lines.

Determining such values is not done easily or quickly. If you have arrived on a campus in what you want to be a leadership role, you must first start with determining these prevailing values. Possibly the major factor about change which planners must recognize is that it must always begin with where you are and not with where you want to go. You cannot go anywhere until you know where you are. This means change in the institutional culture must start with where the values are currently. The first change is from B to C or from 7 to 8. Values, as mentioned above, rarely change from B to F. And values never just go to F or G without awareness of B. You must start by finding B, the starting point, the place where the prevailing values are currently located. Only by starting there (at B) can anyone point a direction and provide leadership.

BUILDING THE CULTURE INTO THE OVERALL PLAN AND STRATEGY

This chapter has attempted to make the case for saying that for any institution in private higher education to plan for its future, it must first determine where it is. Where it is currently is partly a matter of facts such as enrollment, endowment, audit, and other data. These pieces of data are essential for the planning process.

Beyond this, however, is knowing the culture of the institution. To know the culture requires an understanding of the values which permeate the institution. No two institutions are the same. Thus, experience in several other institutions will help only in knowing where to look, what questions to ask. Experience itself will not provide the answers.

Values and the culture it creates are the beginning points for planning. When Columbus started for America, there were many things he did not know and much of which he was unsure, but he did know his starting point and he did know his objective. His objective needed refinement as the voyage developed but he always knew both of these points.

In planning in colleges and universities, both of these must also be known. Where you are both in facts and in your culture (starting with your values) and where you want to go are the essentials.

SUMMARY

Bringing the culture into the planning process, then, begins with identifying the culture. Identifying that culture will portray the possibilities for the mission and vision and thus the present and future of the institution. However, leadership can change culture.

We hope that this chapter has given you some insight into what institutional culture is about and its importance in your planning process.

STUDY QUESTIONS

1. Identify the "core values" of Thorndyke College in the case study in Appendix A.

2. Give an example of how "core values" can be traced to a standard or requirement of an accrediting organization.

Chapter 5

Analysis and Assumptions

The outward-looking character of strategic planning takes into account a growing awareness and significance of the external environment.

–George Keller

A well-defined mission serves as a constant reminder of the need to look outside the institution not only for "customers" but also for measures of success.

–Peter Drucker

This chapter discusses the need to analyze the situation confronting private higher education institutions and to identify any assumptions upon which strategic planning will be based. We will first discuss the need to assess the external environment within which the educational institution operates in order to understand the nature of forces and influences that affect performance and ultimately survival.

Next, we will address the role of internal analysis of the situation within the institution. It is critical that all attributes of the institution be reviewed and understood–internal strengths and weaknesses as well as external opportunities and threats–in order to establish an appropriate basis upon which to conduct strategic planning. At times facts about a key variable are not available (perhaps due to cost or time constraints in collecting the information). Under these conditions, assumptions will be used to fill the "fact gap." Consequently, this step in strategic planning is critical to the success of the process.

EXTERNAL ANALYSIS

It is important to realize that anything that can happen ultimately has a good chance of happening. We truly can have no certain idea what things will be like in the future, in spite of our attempts to predict them. It is vital for the institution to gauge (estimate) the external environment within which it operates. This practice, known as environmental scanning of key factors and trends, should occur on a continuing basis for all institutions. By factors we mean the forces, individuals, and institutions (particularly the competition) which have a current or possible future impact (positive or negative) on the ability of an institution to effectively and efficiently achieve goals, mission and vision.

Institutions continually collect data on changes in their environment at two levels: institutional and school/department. The only way we can effectively manage change is to constantly monitor the environment within which both operate. Examples for private higher education might be the trends in the following list of external environment factors: government, economy, technology, social trends, students, funding, competition, and development in and of other educational institutions (see Step 1 in "Situation Analysis and Assumptions Worksheet" at the end of the chapter for details).

These external environmental factors are studied in the environmental analysis stage. Here is where we look at the past, identify trends, and, in effect, take the pulse of the environment in which the educational institution operates. Environmental analysis and assessment concerns facts, data, and information; it should not be confused with assumptions which are estimates in lieu of the reality of facts.

As an example, an environmental analysis for a four-year college contemplating expansion by way of nontraditional education and/or the addition of graduate programs might include the following factors and trends:

- Educational delivery systems are changing due to changing needs of students coupled with affordable high technology applied to the worldwide information highway known as the Internet.
- The National Association of Students in Higher Education oppose elimination of the subsidies that the government pays

on student loan interest while borrowers are in college (*The Chronicle of Higher Education*, June 16, 1995, Page A28).

- An increasing number of colleges and universities are offering courses and even entire degrees by way of the Internet.
- Education planners, employers, and marketing experts will find useful environmental scan data on historical and projected enrollments. For example, the updated edition of High School Graduates: Projections by State, 1992 to 2009. The report provides actual enrollments and graduate numbers from 1974 to 1992 and projections of graduates through 2009 for all states (*Western Interstate Commission for Higher Education*, Pub. No. 2A239, 52 pp., 1993).
- Mercy College pegs salaries to enrollment. Under a new policy, professors' salaries at Mercy College will rise if student enrollment goes up, and decline if it doesn't. Faculty members approved the plan by a 4-to-1 margin because they did not like the alternative–losing their jobs (*Chronicle of Higher Education*, July 17, 1995).
- The student population is getting older as adults wanting education for personal and/or professional reasons return to higher education.
- The content of college curricula is changing as the "half-life" of information and concepts is getting shorter with the explosion of information and communications.
- The growth of nontraditional programs such as weekend colleges, degree completion programs, and degrees on the Internet will force changes not only in the ways that institutions market themselves but also in the ways in which they function internally.
- There is a movement away from the professor being the center of the teaching/learning process by determining what will be taught and when to offer programs. The movement is toward student-oriented and structured programs designed to meet students' needs, including modular curriculum for all professors to follow and academic policies which are intended to attract and retain students. Thus, a change in the power base on campuses is in process toward greater student control (marketing is of greater importance).

- Strategic alliances within the educational community and between the educational community and industry, government, and management firms will change the way we "think and do" education and training: (1) colleges and universities will share technology and resources, (2) higher education will partner with business and industry in many ways to meet the rapidly changing training needs of the workplace (such as activities of the Council of Adult and Experiential Learning, CAEL), and (3) a greater impact of outside organizations on the campus (see several of the prior items regarding outside organizations).
- Changes in federal financial aid programs will impact certain socioeconomic groups of students.
- Change in the income tax structure will have significant impact on contributions to private higher education.
- Competition from other educational institutions. For example, the establishment of a branch location of an out-of-state university at a local military base may reduce enrollment in certain degree programs. The tendency to operate in a number of locations is becoming more prevalent in both public and private higher education. An institution's geographical territory is no longer protected.
- Lifestyle changes. For example, the percentage of double-income households is increasing with a resulting impact on demand for educational services. On the other hand, an increasing incidence of single-parent households produces an apparent increase in demand for distance education delivery systems.

ASSESSING OPPORTUNITIES AND THREATS

Opportunities and threats related to the external environment are analyzed to determine if any action (strategy) is needed to deal with them. For example, there is a significant growth in what has become known as "degree completion programs" and other nontraditional programs in private higher education at the undergraduate level, a movement primarily of the private sector. Future growth appears to be likely in many areas where such programs do not currently exist. In addition, program students are typically adult learners who, tasting success in completing an undergraduate degree after many years of "stopping out," could be ready to enter a nontraditional or adult learning-oriented program at the graduate level. Alternatively, the institution might decide that, even though the opportunity exists in their community, they do not have the support of some influential stakeholders to pursue nontraditional programs. Opportunities cannot be pursued if they are not recognized, analyzed, and assessed.

The same is true for threats. An educational institution that is not well-financed and is in heavy debt experiences a strong threat when a state-supported institution starts up a branch facility that directly competes with the institution. Also, the institution might risk losing the financial support of existing major donors unless the leadership produces bold new "doable" initiatives that will capture the imaginations of additional donors as well as increase tuition revenue in light of the competitive threat. Recognizing threats and analyzing the possible ramifications of events helps avoid many crises when such recognition can lead to utilizing contingency plans for dealing with such situations. Some have referred to this as "what if" and "what then" analysis. In other words, asking the questions "What if this happens?" and then "What do we do if this happens?" helps an institution deal with major events or factors which might be detrimental to the institution.

External scanning should analyze and assess five factors according to Kaufman and Herman (1991, p. 98):

1. Demographic-related data which concerns the numbers and types of students who attend the college or university. An example of these trends is the change in the age distribution of the student population and its impact on curriculum and degree offerings at the institution.
2. Attitude-related data which allows an assessment of what various influential groups have to say about the current status and future outlook in the education sector: analyzing newspaper and professional reports, listening to conference and media presentations, studying the pronouncements of scholars and blue ribbon study groups, surveying various stakeholders

(alumni, students, donors, and community leaders), and monitoring legislative trends at the federal and state levels.

3. Governmental laws and policy-related data show areas of constraints promulgated by federal, state, and local governments, the courts, and the institution's own board of trustees within which an educational institution must operate. For example, laws and regulations about employment, affirmative action, and the differently-abled impact operations. State government licensing approval of programs and degrees must be reviewed and followed. The increasing tendency of state governments to regulate private higher education means that strategic planning in this sector must consider politics and the general welfare of the citizenry in creating change.

4. Finance-related data–sources of revenues, especially gifts and contributions, must be monitored as they determine the quality and quantity of the educational program. More and more state colleges and universities are strongly pursuing private donations to supplement state appropriations and tuition revenues. Such action is in direct competition with private institutions for donations.

5. Future forecasts and trends–collecting and analyzing data on factors (many factors discussed above) that are critical to the success of the institution, especially in the philanthropic and political arenas.

Another set of external analysis factors is provided below:

1. Economic trends in the locality, the geographic region or student market area, and national and international areas (if applicable). Examples of these trends are changes in personal income (those impacting students' abilities to pay tuition and fees; those impacting institutional expenditures; and those impacting giving patterns), employment, land values, and industry locations.

2. Demographic trends including shifts in age groups, education levels, numbers of broken households (widowed, divorced, single-parent), retired people, and shifts of population to different geographical areas. Also, what are the changes in student/adult learner needs and social values? Are the institu-

tion's services what potential students/adult learners truly need or will want? Apart from basic needs, how well do the institution's services meet students' expectations? What do people in the community surrounding the institution consider to be important? Are the services offered valued by them?

3. Community issues of urban vs. suburban development, growth or decline of commercial activities (including business and government downsizing), transportation, and communication facilities. Changes and innovations in the educational programs and services offered to people in the community. Who is offering them? Are services primarily shifting into governmental hands or private sponsorship? How effective are these services in meeting the needs of the community? What educational programs are proving to be the most popular at this time?

4. Changes in student/adult learner needs and social values. Are your institution's services what your current and potential students/adult learners truly need or will want? Apart from basic needs, how well do the curriculum and current/projected services meet students' expectations? What do people in the institution's community consider to be important? Are the services offered valued by them?

5. Governmental trends impacting student financial aid from governmental sources, trends impacting human resource management issues from governmental regulations such as Americans with Disabilities Act (ADA) and the Equal Employment Opportunities Commission (EEOC).

6. Accreditation agencies and organizations–changes in their standards. Both regional as well as discipline specific accrediting bodies must be considered in the strategic planning process. In fact, many of these organizations are requiring evidence of broad-based strategic planning as part of their criteria for accreditation.

7. Trends in competition from proprietary as well as the public and other private educational institutions for funding, in recruiting faculty and staff, and for programs and services which might overlap. What other things are going on that present the institution with competition at this time?

8. Cultural and social trends that indicate what people value as important, and that logically impact either student recruiting and/or institutional funds development.
9. Technological trends that impact both the way we find and use information as well as those trends that impact how we deliver education and training.

Additional examples of potential external opportunities and threats are listed below:

Potential External Opportunities

- Serve additional student groups in existing market area.
- Geographically diversify into new market areas with branch campuses.
- Diversify into related degree programs.
- Vertically integrate from undergraduate to graduate programs.
- Devise marketing strategies to take advantage of competing educational institutions which are complacent.
- Increase enrollment due to faster growth rate in student markets currently being served.
- Submit proposals to foundations and government agencies which are requesting research proposals in areas of faculty expertise.

Potential External Threats

- Entry of new competitors with lower tuition, perceived higher quality.
- Slower growth rate in student markets currently being served.
- Costly regulatory requirements put into place.
- Changing student needs or tastes.
- Adverse demographic changes.
- Changing giving patterns.

In summary, then, the steps in the process of looking at the external environment include data collection, information analysis, assessment or evaluation, and finally, a process of synthesis leading to the drawing of conclusions about what factors (key success factors) and forces (driving forces) are important input to the strategy-making stage of strategic planning (Chapter 7). Those factors and trends in the external environment (known as opportunities and positive factors/forces) which tend to enhance goal and mission achievement need to be documented, analyzed, and assessed. Of course, the factors and forces that limit and constrain or even threaten goal and mission achievement (known as threats or negative factors/forces) must be noted as well. Implementing the processes of data collection, analysis and assessment is no simple matter because the external environment, over which the institution has little or no control, is continuously changing. New technology, social movements, political changes and pressures, as well as the more commonly recognized economic changes, all create problems and opportunities.

This stage in the strategic planning process does not merely involve gathering data, getting it on paper, and forgetting about it; the environment must be constantly monitored.

INTERNAL ANALYSIS

After you have identified your institution's mission (purpose) and considered the external environment in which it operates, it is important to objectively analyze and assess the strengths and weaknesses of your institution's internal operations. Of the aforementioned institutional analysis method, SWOT (strengths, weaknesses, opportunities, threats), two parts that pertain to internal analysis are strengths and weaknesses. Institutional administrators need to learn from athletic coaches in these areas: coaches are constantly assessing the strengths and weaknesses of their team and of the opponent's. They try to maximize their strengths on game day, and improve on their weaknesses during practice.

At the institution level, another step in a thorough analysis and assessment is a full audit of the institution. A complete study of the institution's emphasis on its educational program, support services, students, faculty, administration, policies, and procedures is needed. Also included in this internal environmental analysis is a study of the management system. (See Step 2 in the worksheet at the end of the chapter.)

Of growing interest is a review called Management Audit in which a consulting firm engages in measuring the effectiveness of the management team. (This is not to be confused with a "management audit" by an accounting firm or an agency reviewing federal financial aid.) The purpose of such an audit is to gather data and to interview people to determine the effectiveness of the leadership, office functions, committee structure, external relations, budget management, personnel issues, compliance with the law and board policy, and other related matters. This could be particularly useful prior to a team visit by an accrediting association in order to have time to make changes prior to that review. It could also be helpful to the institution that is questioning how it will be able to accomplish its mission given the present management team, resources available, and existing external and internal threats.

A questionnaire on both the institution and its management gives administrators information on the effectiveness of the management system and brings major problems to the surface. A method for auditing the strategic planning system is needed. One way of doing this is through a questionnaire reviewing the planning environment, institutional structure, management philosophy and style, planning processes, and other factors relating to the internal institution. The result is a thorough understanding of the strategic planning system. The data collected in the audit can then be analyzed to determine strengths and weaknesses in the institution and its strategic planning system. The key or most important strengths and weaknesses are then included in the strengths and weaknesses part of the strategic planning process.

It is useful to build a database. Of the several types of databases, two are essential: students and donors. The more you know about the people being served, the better you can meet their needs. Many successful businesses, such as Wal-Mart, are continually doing research to learn more about their customers. A private higher education institution should do the same thing. Questions need to be asked and information gathered on such factors as:

- Academic programs (majors by program, student credit hours by program)–on-campus and off-campus if appropriate; non-credit programs

- Faculty and staff (compensation, support, hiring and retaining, satisfaction with the institution)
- Financial affairs (operating budgets, student financial aid)
- Students (demographic information, career plans, satisfaction with academic programs)

All of these are good questions to ask. For example, Thorndyke College (see case study in Appendix A), did a thorough environmental scan and survey of the institution and found that students responded well to recent programmatic changes at the College; however, they were critical about the lack of computer availability at the College.

Robert Cope (1987), in his report entitled "Opportunity from Strength," does a good job of illustrating the use of various strategic planning models with case examples. The document, published by the Association for the Study of Higher Education, also reviews the pre-1987 planning literature and provides both conceptual and practical guidelines along with many fine ideas of collecting, analyzing, and assessing environmental data.

ASSESSING STRENGTHS AND WEAKNESSES

Institutions have certain strengths (core competencies) which make them uniquely suited to carry out their tasks. Conversely, they have certain weaknesses which inhibit their abilities to fulfill their purposes. Like athletic coaches, institutions that hope to achieve their missions and accomplish their tasks need to carefully analyze and assess their strengths and weaknesses and continuously monitor these areas to pick up on changes as they occur.

A complete study of the institution's emphasis on its services and how well they are delivered is the goal. In looking for strengths and weaknesses in the functioning of your institution, a strength is some significant aspect of your operations that is done exceedingly well. What we mean by significant operational aspect is some fundamental activity that is highly likely to affect the performance of your institution in a major way. Conversely, a weakness is some inadequacy in a major activity or resource that reduces the institution's ability to achieve its goals.

Several different benchmarks can be used to identify whether a factor should be considered a strength or a weakness. One internal standard is how well this factor meets its operational goals when compared to other major functions. This comparison can be made over time to establish trends in effectiveness. Another standard is how well the institution handles this factor when compared with this function in other private higher education institutions which might be considered immediate competitors. Another important benchmark for private higher education in particular is how well the activity contributes to the institution's ability to satisfy the expectations of its funding sponsors. But perhaps the most fundamental standard is how well this activity meets the immediate and long-term needs and interests of the traditional and nontraditional learners the institution wishes to serve.

Distinctive Competence

The definitive goal of an internal strengths and weaknesses analysis and assessment is to identify any distinctive competencies. A distinctive competence is some function that we do extraordinarily well. It represents a level of mastery which makes our institution extremely effective in meeting student needs (and possible donor needs) particularly when we consider the typical effectiveness of our competition in this area of operation. In other words, a distinctive competence is a super strength that give us an edge in delivering student satisfaction and making a difference in the lives of students.

There is a lag between performance and reputation. Top level performance by an institution takes a while to become known. Conversely, a fine reputation might help an institution long after its actual performance level has declined.

A systematic way to identify strengths and weaknesses is to divide your institution's operations into major sectors for further analysis and evaluation. Depending on the specific nature of the institution, some basic categories for internal analysis include overall management effectiveness and institutional resources, financial operations, marketing operations, and operations or service functions. A good place to begin is with the management/administration of the institution and its strategic planning systems.

Management and Planning Systems

A specific target of a strengths and weaknesses analysis should be a study of the management system. Management's willingness to take risks, their values, skills, ages, and experience levels are all important aspects of an institution's ability to respond to opportunities. Identifying the effectiveness of the institution's human resources management is also an objective of this portion of the analysis. This can include issues of how well the institution is organized as well as staff turnover and the recruitment and morale of volunteers.

For instance, the demographics of our volunteers are important in understanding volunteer effectiveness. Appropriate questions include the following: How many people do we have in each age group? What are the basic categories of jobs and income levels? What percentage of volunteers consists of retired or widowed persons?

As observers of the higher education scene over several decades, we have noticed that much of the difference between institutions in their management and strategic planning systems is something that might be called the "courage factor." The management of many institutions is marked by very low courage. These are the institutions which are destined to be the followers. It is a comfortable place, it appears, for many management teams in private higher education. The resulting institutions are not very exciting, but they are largely predictable. Those institutions with a higher "courage factor" are those marked with creativity, risk, new ideas, service to students, a bright outlook on the future, and excellence. They make more mistakes, but they have more successes as well.

Still another target for analysis and evaluation concerns our institution's culture or personality. The following questions deal with our institutional culture profile:

1. Are we outgoing and proactive in our service philosophy? For example, if we have a number of adult evening students on our campus who find it difficult to come in during the day, do we have evening office hours, or are evening appointments available? Is the library open 12 months of the year if we have

students 12 months of the year, or do we close at certain times to facilitate vacations for librarians?

2. Are we student/adult learner driven or do we focus more on financial sponsors' expectations? Do we know what our students want and what they need? An unidentified student need is seldom met.

3. Does our institution collaborate with other community agencies and institutions? Does the president get together with other presidents, the deans with deans from other institutions?

4. As a part of private higher education, what are our primary interests and social values? When was the last time we made an effort to assess this?

5. What is the power structure of our institution? Who makes the decisions and by what process? Is this process effective in meeting our mission?

Also important to analyze is the effectiveness of our present programs. What are they? Is the leadership for each program effective? How much interest and support does each program have? How effective is it in use of allocated resources? A management questionnaire can be developed which provides information on the effectiveness of the management system in the various programs and brings major problems and opportunities to the surface.

Another target of this analysis is the strategic planning system. Is strategic planning undertaken systematically and performed on a regular basis? Are contingency plans considered? Are the plans realistic? Are they in fact used? All are important issues. Again, a questionnaire can be used to identify and review the strategic planning environment and process, institutional structure, and management philosophy and style as it relates to strategic planning and to other planning factors relating to the institution's performance.

The result is a thorough understanding of the strategic planning system. The data collected in the audit can then be analyzed to determine strengths and weaknesses in the strategic planning system. The most important are then included in a strengths and weaknesses summary as a portion of the overall strategic audit. In a similar fashion, the following sectors can be analyzed using surveys and the major findings incorporated into the audit.

Financial Resources

The total amount of financial resources an institution has available and the process through which these funds are allocated influence the institution's ability to function effectively. For some institutions there are insurmountable financial barriers. Not only are capital needs extensive, but other expenditures are at a high level. Adequate financial resources must be available to ensure the provision of adequate production and marketing capabilities or the institution must have easy access to funding sources before some opportunities can be undertaken.

Adequate initial financial resources are needed to operate (in many cases) for the first few years while enough students or funding sponsors are developed to sustain an operation. Low revenue levels and high operating costs during the first few years must be anticipated. It goes without saying that unless the financial resources to permit continued operation are available, failure can be anticipated. Thus, an institution's current financial position plus its ability to successfully obtain financing directly influence its ability to pursue opportunities.

Specifically, financial resources of the institution, including operating funds, special funds, donations, and expenditures, should be analyzed. Appropriate questions include the following: What has been our performance over the last five years in adhering to budget limits? What is our ability to raise funds when needed? Other specific targets for analysis include break-even points, cash flow, and debt-to-asset ratios.

Marketing Resources

An institution's ability to take advantage of opportunities requires personnel with the marketing skills necessary to develop and execute effective marketing strategies (see Chapter 7). A good service does not guarantee success. The old adage "Build a better mousetrap and the world will beat a path to your door" is just not true without effective marketing. An institution must get its message across if it is to thrive.

This requires good marketing, and good marketing is the result of the work of good marketers. Many institutions that were successful in previous time periods have failed in the new environment because of a lack of current marketing know-how. If an institution does not have adequate marketing skills available within its own institution, its financial resources must be sufficient to acquire the marketing personnel and/or training combined with consulting assistance.

Operations/Services Resources

Several distinctly different production resource elements affect an institution's ability to handle new opportunities–service capacity, cost structure, technology, and personnel skills. Capacity to provide services is influenced by previous commitments to acquire facilities. In the short run, this capacity is usually fixed, but it can be altered, over time, for new strategic opportunities. The skills of faculty and staff available during the short run are also considered fixed. Therefore, an institution must have both the capacity and the skills on hand or it must have the financial ability to acquire them. The cost structure of an institution can be a determining factor for some opportunities. The ability or lack of ability to deliver services in a cost-efficient manner can determine an institution's staying power.

Technological capabilities must also be considered. Some new services may require technology not currently available in the organization. If the technology cannot be acquired at a reasonable cost, some opportunities might have to be foregone. Educational technology, either owned or having it accessible, is becoming a necessity in many institutions.

Some appropriate equipment and space questions include the following: Are equipment and space adequate for present needs and for planned future needs? Are they in good operating condition? Are they costly to maintain or operate? To what extent are they "state of the art?" What plans are there for replacement/upgrading?

Additional Factors

Factors that are distinctively educationally specific at the institutional level or the school/department level and which must be collected by the institution itself include:

- Enrollment (inquiries, applications, matriculants, retention)
- Tuition and Fees
- Student Financial Aid (external aid, discounts, and waivers)
- Institutional Advancement (institutional image, contributions, deferred giving, endowment, alumni giving, capital projects, deferred maintenance)
- Educational Quality (reports of reviews of instructional programs, accreditation reports, job placements of graduates, student surveys of instructional quality)

It is relatively easy to identify the strengths in each of these areas. When you attempt to define weaknesses, it becomes a little more painful. Often, institutions must call in outside consultants to be able to candidly pinpoint their limitations along with their opportunities. But weaknesses and limitations must be recognized before you move on. The process should result in all the evaluations listed in the internal analysis being separated into strengths and weaknesses. Each institution will have a unique set of potential and actual internal strengths. Some of them are:

Potential Internal Strengths

- Core competencies in key disciplines; recognized by peers and general public
- Adequate financial resources as evidenced in endowment and scholarships
- Well-thought-of by students/contributors
- An acknowledged educational leader
- Well-conceived school/department strategies
- Insulated from strong competitive pressures
- Cost advantages
- Ability to move quickly to seize opportunities (lack of bureaucratic barriers)
- Some professors hold leadership positions in their professional associations
- Proven administration (management team) and board of trustees
- Identified opportunities which fit within the mission of the institution

Potential Internal Weaknesses

Each institution also has a unique set of potential internal weaknesses. Some of them might be:

- No clear strategic direction; fuzzy mission, unfocused strategies
- Financial problems; consistent excess expenditures over revenues
- Missing key competencies
- Obsolete, inefficient, or high maintenance facilities and equipment
- Poor track record in implementing strategies
- Plagued with bureaucratic inefficiencies and bottlenecks
- Set of majors and/or degree programs too narrow
- Unable to finance needed changes in strategy
- Alumni support for the institution has not been well organized resulting in below average giving and student recruiting
- Within the next ten years, 50 percent of the institution's senior professors will retire
- People have little faith in the ability of the institution to meet student needs
- The institution has experienced a 25 percent vacancy rate in dormitories causing a drain on general fund revenues

It is suggested that a strategic planning team (group) identify strengths first and display them for group review. Through discussions, the group might then agree on perhaps five major strengths. They then might have each person write down on paper two or three weaknesses of the institution, which are displayed for group review to generate discussion. Only with an objective appraisal of strengths and weaknesses can realistic objectives be set.

MAKING ASSUMPTIONS

The next step is to make your major assumptions. These should be made about spheres over which you have little or absolutely no control (i.e., the external environment). One good place to start is to extend some of the items studied in the external analysis. Using the environmental trends for a private higher education institution noted earlier, assumptions for planning and management of your institution might well include such statements as those listed below:

1. The average price of college tuition will not increase more that 3 percent per year for the next five years.
2. Intervention by the federal government in student financial aid will continue to escalate. Some significant changes in the federal component of financial aid will be mandated by Congress within five years.
3. Philanthropy in private higher education will grow, in the aggregate, at a rate equal to or greater than the rate of inflation.
4. Technological advances and their application to education will continue at an ever-increasing pace. Many advances will continue to be expensive, but others will represent competition to traditional on-campus services.
5. The growth, applicability, and accessibility of the Internet (information highway) will continue into the foreseeable future. Increasingly, it will have an impact on how we teach and deliver education in the United States and around the world.
6. The value of life-long learning will increase resulting in increased demand for training and education.
7. Changes in the demographic and/or psychographic structure of the population will require new types of degrees and courses.
8. During the next five years, it is likely that other colleges, either private or public, will increase their presence in our market area—either through a branch location nearby, a nontraditional program, or through some form of distance education delivery system.

A list should be developed of certain assumptions that characterize strategic aspects of your institution's operation. Assumptions are those situational trends that, by your estimate, will significantly impact your institution's activities during the strategic planning period. Major considerations include the nature of your students' expectations, your funding sources, and the nature of competition. Although these assumptions are outside your control, they are basic beginning points for the educational institution's plans for future delivery of services.

Here are some possible assumptions that fit the strategic planning model:

1. Quality leads to quantity. The quality of service leads to expansion of services. Higher quality of services leads to greater demand for services.
2. A commitment to excellence produces confidence in the institution's leadership and management. If the administration (management team) is committed to excellence and demonstrates it in its leadership style, then the faculty and staff will feed off this confidence allowing them to persevere in uncertain situations.
3. Sponsorship and funding of the institution will continue to be a challenge, but continued effort will produce sources of funds, sometimes from new and unexpected directions.
4. Each service offered has some unique aspects to it that might require new ways of doing things. Policies and procedures should be adapted to produce the best results, not just standardization.

Assumptions must be directly related to action. Note the relationship between assumption and proposed action in the following example:

> *Assumption:* Despite changes in types of courses, degrees, and in how education is delivered, an accredited degree from the United States will continue to be much sought after and valuable especially in the minds of the international community.
>
> To deal with declining enrollment at your college, an expansion plan is based in part on the external analysis that has been thoroughly examined. In this case, you see there is an opportunity to serve international students by developing a presence in their own country–say Singapore. Then you base your plan on an assumption. You either assume demand by foreign students for an accredited United States institution or you do not. How does this translate into action?
>
> *Action:* Negotiate a strategic alliance with a local Singapore institution that can supply the services and resources to complement your expansion plan.

The key is knowing what is going on and being alert to opportunities. Then develop a full plan based on a few realistic assumptions. If an assumption changes, then the plan changes.

The worksheet at the end of this chapter is a useful tool for internal and external analysis. Answering all the questions can be a good start in assessing the institution in several areas.

SUMMARY

This chapter has emphasized the importance of coming to grips with the external and internal environments in which you must work to fulfill your mission. Minimizing weaknesses and capitalizing on strengths helps bolster the ability of an institution to operate in its external environment. Specifying the assumptions provides a basis for thoughtful consideration of the basic premises on which you operate. They should also cause you to ponder the "What if, What then" scenarios that help avoid disruptions in the institution's operations through strategic planning.

SITUATION ANALYSIS AND ASSUMPTIONS WORKSHEET

This worksheet will aid you in completing a Strengths, Weaknesses, Opportunities, and Threats (SWOT) analysis.

I. **Step 1. External Environment Analysis:** From community, industry, or institutional surveys and your own sources of information, take your institution's pulse. You are looking for trends–what is going on now and how this relates to past trends that have influenced your institution's performance. From this analysis, list key opportunities and threats for each of the following environmental sectors:

    A. Government

        Opportunities

           1.

           2.

           3.

        Threats

           1.

           2.

           3.

    B. Economy

        Opportunities

           1.

           2.

           3.

        Threats

           1.

           2.

           3.

C. Technology

Opportunities

   1.

   2.

   3.

Threats

   1.

   2.

   3.

D. Social Trends

Opportunities

   1.

   2.

   3.

Threats

   1.

   2.

   3.

E. Students

Opportunities

   1.

   2.

   3.

Threats

   1.

   2.

   3.

F. Funding Sources/Sponsorship

Opportunities

1.

2.

3.

Threats

1.

2.

3.

G. Competing Educational Institutions

Opportunities

1.

2.

3.

Threats

1.

2.

3.

Next, **evaluate your external analysis:**

- Have you listed several international/national trends that affect your institution?

_____

_____

_____

- Have you listed several local trends that affect your institution?

_____

_____

_____

• Have you identified trends unique to your institution?

_____

_____

_____

• Have you listed several of your most important competitors? What is distinctive about them?

_____

_____

_____

• Which competitors are growing, becoming stronger?

_____

_____

_____

• Which competitors are declining?

_____

_____

_____

• What are the successful ones doing to cause their growth/vibrancy?

_____

_____

_____

II. **Step 2. Internal Operations Analysis:** Using the question guides below and your own information, list key strengths and weaknesses for each of the following sectors of your institution's operations:

  A. Management and Planning Systems

   1. Use these questions to help you prepare your strengths and weaknesses list for the management and planning systems portion of your institution's operation:

• Do you have a strategic planning system?

_____

_____

_____

• How does it work?

_____

_____

_____

• Is the institutional structure of your institution allowing effective use of resources?

_____

_____

_____

• Is control centralized or decentralized?

_____

_____

_____

• Are performance measures and information system controls in evidence? What are they?

_____

_____

_____

• What staffing needs do you have?

_____

_____

_____

- Is there a motivation problem? Is it centered in one segment of the institution or is it broadly felt?

_____

_____

_____

- Is your current strategy defined? Is it based upon a strategic plan? Is it working?

_____

_____

_____

- How efficient are operations? Where could improvements be made?

_____

_____

_____

- What is your synopsis of the current management situation? How strong is the management team? Are there obvious weaknesses?

_____

_____

_____

2. Now list the strengths and weaknesses of your management and planning systems:

  - Strengths

_____

_____

_____

- Weaknesses

_____

_____

_____

B. Financial Resources

1. Use these questions to help you prepare your strengths and weaknesses list for the financial portion of your institution's operation:

   - Describe the current financial situation of the institution (number of years operating in the black, current year status, debt load relative to assets and ability to retire debt, whether debt is declining or increasing, any financial statements of the institution, comments of accrediting institutions).

   _____

   _____

   _____

   - Do you have regular financial statements prepared? (How complete are they, are they accurate, are they ready by the 15th of the month following, are they distributed on timely bases to everyone having approval authority for an account?)

   _____

   _____

   _____

- What tools would be beneficial in the analysis? (year to date, comparison to a year ago, trends, debt analysis, income analysis, expenditure analysis, comparison to budget)?

_____

_____

_____

- Do you have pro forma statements (see Appendix C) for revenue centers, such as each department/school, etc.?

_____

_____

_____

2. Now list the strengths and weaknesses of your financial resources:

   - Strengths

   _____

   _____

   _____

   - Weaknesses

   _____

   _____

   _____

C. Marketing Resources

   1. Use these questions to help you prepare your strengths and weaknesses list for the marketing portion of your institution's operation:

- Does the institution have established written marketing policies?

_____

_____

_____

- Have you established a written marketing plan outlining what you will and will not do?

_____

_____

_____

- Have you identified your potential students in the written marketing plan?

_____

_____

_____

- Have you identified your funding sponsors (beyond tuition)?

_____

_____

_____

- What are your competitors' services and products, level of demand, and relative market positions?

_____

_____

_____

• What is the structure of tuition and fees charged? How competitive is it?

_____

_____

_____

• What promotional activities (advertising, recruitment strategy) is the institution using? Are there written goals? Is there an advertising budget?

_____

_____

_____

• What is your synopsis of the current marketing situation? How well does the marketing compare to the competition?

_____

_____

_____

2. Now list the strengths and weaknesses of your marketing resources:

• Strengths

_____

_____

_____

• Weaknesses

_____

_____

_____

D. Operations or Services Resources

   1. Use these questions to help you prepare your strengths and weaknesses list for the operations or services portion of your institution:

     • What are your operations capacities? (How many students can enroll in your facilities, how many students can be housed and fed, what is an acceptable rate of use?)

_____

_____

_____

     • What is the age and condition of your facilities?

_____

_____

_____

     • What is the age and serviceability of existing equipment (including computers)?

_____

_____

_____

     • What quality control systems are in place?

_____

_____

_____

2. Now list the strengths and weaknesses of your operations or services resources:

- Strengths

_____

_____

_____

- Weaknesses

_____

_____

_____

Next, **evaluate your internal analysis:**

- How many students are you currently serving? (How does this compare to a year ago, a term ago, three years ago?)

_____

_____

_____

III. **Step 3: Development of Assumptions:** List the major assumptions on which the strategic plan is based.

1. _____

_____

2. _____

_____

3. _____

_____

4. _____

_____

5. _____

_____

Chapter 6

Establishing Objectives
and Key Result Areas

The purpose of developing a clear set of institutional goals is precisely to keep the institution from drifting into an uncertain future.

—Philip Kotler
Marketing Professor and Consultant
to Educational Institutions

When you are clear about your mission, corporate goals and operating objectives flow from it.

—Frances Hesselbein
Former Executive Director,
Girl Scouts of America

The best definitions of mission are operational. They lead to goals that tell people what to do and very often how to do it.

—Peter Drucker

In this chapter we will discuss establishing objectives, the third step in the strategic planning process. After the purpose or mission of the educational institution has been defined, internal and external analysis/assessment completed, and assumptions made, then—and only then—can relevant objectives be considered.

Clearly, one cannot achieve goals if none exist. Although this idea is quite simple, many people overlook it. In order to accomplish anything, we must make up our minds to do it. If we fail to do this first step, we simply waste our time and energy by going in circles. Later, we look back at what we accomplished and wonder where the time went.

NATURE AND ROLE OF OBJECTIVES

The concepts–Key Result Areas, goals, objectives, and targets– are often used synonymously when talking about long-term and short-term objectives designed to implement a mission statement. Whatever the label used, the idea is to focus on a specific set of target activities, end-results, and/or outcomes to be accomplished. Think of the analogy of the archer used earlier. A college administrator wants the whole institution aimed at the same target just as an archer wants his arrow aimed at the bulls-eye. However, that target might include a number of different but mission-related elements that clearly reflect institutional direction. People get confused and disorganized if they do not know where they are going. The success or failure of an institution in private higher education is based on its ability to set and implement plans to achieve goals, as well as on tools with which to measure progress.

Kotler and Murphy (1990) advocate a hierarchical approach in setting overall goals which then progresses throughout various levels with increasingly specific but congruent objectives. The implication here is that strategic overall direction is driven by the mission as interpreted by senior leadership of the institution, but much latitude is given for input at lower levels.

For the purposes of this book, we will use the following terms: "Key Result Areas" are an institution's general topic of action in its strategic plan; within each Key Result Area, there are "objectives"– the specific areas of action–and "strategies"–the detailed activities that implement those areas of action.

Setting Clear Objectives

Effective administration and successful strategic planning require clarity and focus. Of course, the mission statement (purpose) of the institution is the starting point to meet these criteria.

Likewise, clarity and focus must persist in setting and communicating objectives and Key Result Areas of the institution.

There are a number of reasons why private higher education institutions fail to set clear objectives:

1. Many educational leaders and managers fear accountability.
2. Many projects continue even when they no longer serve an institution's goals.
3. Private higher education institutions often undertake any activity for which funding becomes available.
4. Some administrators fear hard-nosed evaluation might undermine humanitarian instincts among the faculty and staff.
5. Private higher education administrators must spend a great deal of time on activities that do not immediately further their mission-directed goals (meeting with donors, fund raising, explaining vision/mission, etc.).
6. Many private higher education institutions do not have a management-oriented financial report card to tell them how they are doing (Harvey and Sander, 1987).
7. A lack of understanding of the need for strategic planning.
8. A lack of understanding of how to proceed with the strategic planning process.
9. The absence of a high "courage factor."

As objectives are established in the institution, some of those obstacles mentioned above might not be applicable. However, most of this list could be applied in any type of institutional setting.

College- or university-wide objectives are broad statements which are not necessarily measurable but meet four criteria:

1. congruent with the vision/mission of the institution,
2. provide clear targets or end-results to which school/department level objectives relate,
3. provide fixed responsibilities of who is responsible for implementing each of the items, and
4. provide a timetable by which each of the items is expected to be accomplished.

These lower level objectives are clear, concise, written statements outlining what is to be accomplished in key areas within a certain time period and in objectively measurable terms.

Types of Objectives

Objectives can be classified as routine, problem-solving, innovative, team, personal, and budget performance. Drucker (1954, p. 102) states that "objectives are not fate; they are direction. They are not commands, but they are commitments. They do not determine the future, but they are the means by which the resources and energies of the operation can be mobilized for the making of the future."

Examples of these classifications at the individual and department level of a private higher education institution might be:

ROUTINE. Seventy-five percent of each entering class will take five years or less to complete a baccalaureate program.

PROBLEM SOLVING. Given the increasing incidence of writing problems among entering students, a remedial writing lab will be established and staffed with the objective of raising grammar and spelling competency by two levels over the next two years, as measured by the institution's currently adopted grammar/spelling computerized programs.

INNOVATIVE. By the end of the current academic year, each full-time faculty member will be trained and supported to develop at least one out-of-session assignment requiring students to use and document the use of the Internet.

TEAM. During the fall semester, the graduate teaching faculty will team up to produce at least five measurable outcomes with evidence of mission congruence for the newly approved MA degree in the School of Education.

PERSONAL. During the next academic year, each full-time faculty will produce and implement a professional development plan which includes measurable minimal competencies in computer literacy.

BUDGET PERFORMANCE. Each department/unit of the institution will produce an approved budget which uses not only the format developed for the institution, but also a second format that shows how specific elements in the unit's strategic plan will be financed within the approved overall unit budget.

Objectives can be set at upper institutional levels in Key Result Areas such as growth, finances, physical resources, staff development, and attitudes. They are also needed in subunits, departments, or divisions of an institution. Most important, all institutional objectives must be consistent and linked to the purpose/mission statement(s). Thus, a department's objectives should lead to accomplishing the overall institution's goals, which should correspond to the purpose/mission of the college/university. (An example of setting objectives and how they might be related between two levels of an educational institution is illustrated later in this chapter: see under "Student Objectives" in the section "Key Result Areas in a Strategic Plan.")

Purpose of Objectives

Objectives serve three fundamental purposes. First, they serve as a road map. Objectives are the measurable results desired upon completion of the planning period. In the absence of objectives, no sense of direction can be attained in decision making. In planning, objectives answer two of the basic questions posed in the planning process: Where do we want to go? What do we want to accomplish?

A second basic purpose served by objectives is in the evaluation of performance. The objectives in the strategic plan become the yardsticks used to evaluate performance. As will be pointed out later, it is impossible to evaluate performance without some standard by which results can be compared. The objectives become the standards for evaluating actual performance because they are the statements of results desired by the planner.

A third purpose served by objectives is that they become the focal point for strategy decisions. As will later be discussed in detail in Chapter 7, strategy is the process of making and implementing action plans to go from where we are today (current situational analysis) to where we want to be (objectives).

Objectives have sometimes been called the neglected area of management. In many situations there is a failure to set objectives, or the objectives which are set forth are unsound and therefore lose much of their effectiveness. To counteract this, management tools and systems, including one called management by objectives (MBO) and another called total quality management (TQM), have been developed. While each of these systems has its own identity and elements, they both emphasize the need for setting objectives as a basic managerial process, providing coordination of activities at all levels of the institution. Related to this is the current interest in "reengineering" whereby an organization reevaluates everything it does in the perspective of its mission (Hammer and Stanton, 1995).

For the administrator in private higher education, the application of objectives in the strategic planning process translates into four basic steps (Muczyk and Reimann, 1989). First, the administrator sits down with each of the staff and mutually works out objectives that each staff member will pursue in the assigned area of responsibility. These objectives should support the overall objectives, goals, and mission established by the institution. Each of the staff members with supervisory responsibilities, in turn, holds similar meetings with his or her staff or volunteers. These meetings should be held at each management level so that objectives are fully coordinated.

Second, in addition to objective-setting at these meetings, strategies or descriptions of actions to be taken to accomplish each objective should be laid out. Third, follow-up meetings should be held periodically to monitor progress toward objectives, identify problems, and mutually determine methods to correct any difficulties. The final step involves an overall evaluation of goal accomplishment for individuals and units at year's end or the end of the planning period. From this, new objectives for the coming planning period can be determined.

ALTERNATIVES TO MANAGING BY OBJECTIVES

One way to be convinced of the usefulness and power of managing by objectives is to consider some of the alternatives (Thompson and Strickland, 1986, p. 52):

1. *Managing by Extrapolation (MBE)*. This approach relies on the principle "If it ain't broke, don't fix it." The basic idea is to keep on doing about the same things in about the same ways because what we're doing (1) works well enough and (2) has gotten us where we are. The basic assumption is that, for whatever reason, "Our act is together, so why worry? The future will take care of itself and things will work out all right."

2. *Managing by Crisis (MBC)*. This approach to administration is based upon the idea that the strength of any really good manager is in solving problems. Since there are plenty of crises around–enough to keep everyone occupied–managers ought to focus their time and energy on solving the most pressing problems of today. MBC is, essentially, reactive rather than proactive, and the events that occur dictate management decisions.

3. *Managing by Subject (Area) (MBS)*. The MBS approach occurs when no institution-wide consensus or clear-cut directives exist on which way to head and what to do. Each manager translates this to mean "do your best to accomplish what you think should be done." This is a "do your own thing the best way you know how" approach. This is also referred to as "the mystery approach." Managers are left on their own with no clear direction ever articulated by senior management.

4. *Managing by Hope (MBH)*. In this approach, decisions are predicated on the hope that they will work out and that good times are just around the corner. It is based on the belief that if you try hard enough and long enough, then things are bound to get better. Poor performance is attributed to unexpected events and the fact that decisions always have uncertainties and surprises. Much time, therefore, is spent hoping and wishing things will get better.

All four of these approaches represent "muddling through." Absent is any effort to calculate what effort is needed to influence where an institution is headed and what its activities should be to reach specific objectives. In contrast, managing by objectives is much more likely to achieve targeted results and have a sense of direction.

CHARACTERISTICS OF GOOD OBJECTIVES

For an objective to accomplish its purpose of providing direction and a standard for evaluation, it must possess certain characteristics. The more these attributes are possessed by a given objective, the more likely it will achieve its basic purpose. Sound objectives should have the following characteristics:

1. *Objectives should be clear and concise.* There should not be any room for misunderstanding in what results are sought in a given objective. The use of long statements with words or phrases which may be defined or interpreted in different ways by different people should be avoided.
2. *Objectives should be in written form.* This helps solve two problems: unclear, ineffective communication and alteration of unwritten objectives over time. Everyone realizes that oral statements can be unintentionally altered as they are communicated. Written statements avoid this problem and permit ease of communication. A second problem involves the tendency to want to "look good," often at the expense of actual performance. Unwritten objectives can be altered to fit current circumstances.
3. *Objectives should name specific results in Key Result Areas.* The key areas in which objectives are needed were identified earlier. Specific desired results, such as $100,000 in annual contributions rather than a "high level of contributions" or "an acceptable level of contributions," should be used to avoid doubt about what result is sought.
4. *Objectives should be stated for a specific time period.* Objectives can be set for a short run, or an immediate time period such as six months to one year. Building on longer time frames, accomplishment of short-term objectives should serve as segments of a successful completion of longer-term objectives. The time period specified becomes a deadline for producing results and also sets up the final evaluation of the success of a strategy.
5. *Objectives should be stated in measurable terms.* Concepts that defy precise definition and qualification should be avoided. "Goodwill" is an example of a concept that is impor-

tant, but which in itself is difficult to define and measure. If a planner felt goodwill was a concept which needed to be measured, a substitute measure or measures would have to be used. An objective related to goodwill which would be capable of quantification might be stated as follows: "To have at least 85 percent of our students rate our educational institution as the best in the area in our annual survey." Phrases such as "improve alumni relations" not only are not clear or specific, but also are statements which cannot be measured. What does "improve" mean? Increase the number of contacts during the year? If the statement is quantified as "Call every known alumni at least once a year prior to the annual alumni fundraising effort for the purpose of completing a questionnaire to learn how the institution might serve them," it can be objectively measured. The accomplishment or failure of such a stated objective can be readily evaluated.

6. *Objectives at each administrative level must be consistent with overall institutional objectives and purpose.* This idea has been previously stated but must be continually reemphasized because of the need for institutional unity and focus which contributes to effectiveness, efficiency, and excellence.

7. *Objectives should be attainable but of sufficient challenge to stimulate effort.* A problem can be avoided if this characteristic is achieved. The institution should avoid the frustration produced by objectives which cannot be attained, or which cannot be attained within the specified time period. For instance, large percentage increases in scores on professional license examinations can be unrealistic as objectives if an institution's average pass rate is significantly low. Take the fields of accounting, counseling, or education: each of these professions have national examinations which are necessary to pass in order to receive a license to practice. If, for example, the pass rate for education majors on the national examination is far below average, it would be unrealistic to increase the pass rate from 35 percent to 75 percent in only one year. The desirability and likelihood of substantial increases become doubtful. Perhaps a challenging, yet realistic objective would

be to consistently increase the pass rate 5 percent each year for the next seven years.

8. *Objectives should clearly indicate the person or persons who are responsible for the implementation of the objective on a quality and timely basis.* Everyone's job is no person's job. When responsibility is fixed, the person (or persons) has greater freedom to move ahead due to the clarity in his or her mind as well as those around the issue. It also gives greater visibility as to where the pressure needs to go if the project is not getting done properly or on a timely basis.

There could be a problem in setting objectives which are so easy to attain that only minimum effort is needed. This results in performance evaluations that look good from a distance since every goal is being accomplished but that, in reality, serve only to camouflage lackluster performance well short of the potential. Easy goals fail to maximize the contribution of a given strategic plan.

One approach to writing objectives which contain realistic, but challenging characteristics is to apply a set of criteria to each statement to increase the probability of good objectives. One such list follows:

1. *Relevance.* Are the objectives related to and supportive of the basic purpose of the institution?
2. *Practicality.* Do the objectives take into consideration obvious constraints (such as budgetary limitations)?
3. *Challenge.* Do the objectives provide a challenge?
4. *Measurability.* Are the objectives capable of some form of quantification, if only on an order of magnitude basis?
5. *Schedule.* Are the objectives so constituted that they can be time phased and monitored at interim points to ensure progress toward their attainment?
6. *Balance.* Do the objectives provide for a proportional emphasis on all activities and keep the strengths and weaknesses of the institution in proper balance?

Objectives that meet such criteria are much more likely to serve their intended purposes and facilitate clear communications. The resulting statements can then serve as the directing force in the development of strategy. Consider the following examples of poorly stated objectives with remarks to suggest a better statement:

Poor: Our objective is to maximize student learning.

(How much is "maximum?" The statement is not subject to measurement. What criterion or yardstick will be used to determine if and when actual levels of achievement are equal to the maximum? In addition, no deadline is specified.)

Better: Our objective is to achieve learning outcomes such that 90 percent of graduates will pass the state licensure examination on the first attempt.

Poor: Our objective is to increase contributions of first-time givers.

(How much? A $1 increase will meet that objective, but is that really the desired target?)

Better: Our objective during this calendar year is to increase donations from first-time givers from $300,000 to $350,000.

Poor: Our objective is to boost the student recruiting advertising budget by 15 percent.

(Advertising is an activity, not a result. The advertising objective should be stated in terms of what result the extra advertising is intended to produce.)

Better: Our objective is to boost enrollment by 10 percent in each of the next five years with the help of a 15 percent annual increase in advertising expenditures.

Poor: Our objective is to be the best educational institution of its type in our area.

(Not specific enough; what measures of "best" are to be used? Number of students served? Level of endowment? Number of new programs started? Services offered? Faculty/student ratio?)

Better: We will strive to become the number-one private higher education institution of its kind in the metropolitan area in terms of the percentage of students graduated within five years of matriculation.

The following practical suggestions are offered for writing objectives:

1. Objectives should start with the word "to" followed by an action verb, since the achievement of an objective must come as a result of specific action.
2. Each objective should specify a single major result to be accomplished so the group will know precisely when the objective has been achieved.
3. An objective should have a target date for accomplishment.
4. The objective should relate directly to the mission statement of the group or individual. A department or school should not write an objective outside the scope of its own mission statement or one that pertains more to the mission statement of the college/university. This might seem obvious, but groups often commit themselves to projects with outcomes for which they have neither responsibility nor authority.
5. The objective must be understandable to those who will be working to achieve the specified results.
6. An objective must be possible to achieve.
7. The objective should be consistent with board-approved, institution-wide policies and practices.

KEY RESULT AREAS IN A STRATEGIC PLAN

Objectives should be established in *all* Key Result Areas of operations. Key Result Areas are those activities which are most likely to impact the performance of the institution. They are the few things that must go right if the institution is to be effective and thrive. For private higher education institutions, objectives should be set for the following "Key Result Areas":

1. Level of enrollment
2. Level and sources of funds (budget compliance)
3. Student acceptance

4. Quality of programs
5. Quantity/type of programs appropriate to those being served
6. Leadership effectiveness
7. Quantity and quality of services
8. Endowment development
9. Strategic planning

"The institution cannot successfully pursue all objectives in each of the above nine result areas simultaneously because of a limited budget and various tradeoffs, such as between increased cost efficiency and improved classroom teaching" (Kotler and Murphy 1990, pp. 239-252). However, on an ongoing basis, these result areas and their related measurable objectives must be reviewed and discussed as to priority, effectiveness, and congruence with the mission statement.

Strategic plans for educational institutions usually focus on at least three key result areas: students, educational program, and contributions. Short-term objectives are stated for the operating period only, normally one year; whereas long-term objectives usually span three to 20 years. The desirable outcome of bringing focus to the activities of an institution through the strategic planning process necessitates the need for congruence among the mission statement and objective statements in Key Result Areas.

Student Objectives

Student objectives (outcomes) are critical to a number of key institutional stakeholders–prospective students, accreditation agencies, alumni, community, and others. All of these constituents are concerned about job placement in the short run and achieving the institution's mission in the long run. Objectives guide in decisions about the educational program, its curriculum, and academic/administrative support systems. A list of general student outcome categories includes enrollment management (student recruitment, admissions, retention), graduation, placement, performance on job, and student satisfaction. Examples at yet another level of detail of student outcome objectives are:

1. Degrees and certificates earned by an entering class (cohort) of students

2. Length of time to program completion
3. Educational program "stopouts" or dropouts
4. Students working toward and receiving additional degrees and certificates
5. Student ability to transfer credits
6. Level of achievement of former students in another institution
7. Percentage of graduates successful in obtaining preferred first job
8. Performance of student on the job from employer's perspective

Student objectives are especially important in providing direction to the development of the strategy section of the plan. As shown in Exhibit 6.1, they specify results desired for students by program category. Student objectives should have the same characteristics as other objectives. They must be stated in objectively measurable terms and should be evaluated in relation to their accomplishment as a part of the monitoring and control system used in the plan.

Academic Program Objectives

The central purpose of the institution is the education of its students, even though a variety of delivery systems might be employed. Academic program objectives also serve as enabling objectives in faculty in support personnel and in funding decisions and planning. Examples of these objectives are provided in the following general list: student knowledge and skills, curriculum, faculty (teaching, research, and community service), faculty satisfaction, academic support (especially library and computer areas), and administrative support.

Accreditation agencies are becoming increasingly interested in the quality of education and the institution's integrity. This takes the context of answering in an objective manner the penetrating ques-

Exhibit 6.1. Examples of Student Objectives

1. Achieve a level of 3,000 enrollment by the year (year), which requires an average rate of growth of 9 percent per year.
2. Achieve placement for graduates in the field of study at a level comparable to other educational institutions in our market area.

tion: "How well are we doing in accordance with what we said we would do as revealed in written advertising, brochures, and the catalog?" The whole area of institutional effectiveness has as its underpinnings the principles and practices of strategic planning and evaluation discussed throughout this book. As shown in Exhibit 6.2, academic program objectives specify results desired of faculty, staff, and administration.

Financial and Development Objectives

Contributions and cost control objectives represent sound organizational management practices and are a vital part of any educational institution. While they are never ends in themselves, they are the enabling resources and procedures that are essential for effective and efficient performance of the institution. However, there is a more practical reason for including specific statements in these areas:

- Contributions objectives force the planner to estimate the resources needed to underwrite specific educational programs and services to students and all the other stakeholders.
- Cost/expense objectives require the planner to develop program-related budgets in addition to budgets using a chart of accounts to meet the needs of the auditor and the Internal Revenue Service.

Exhibit 6.2. Examples of Academic Program Objectives

1. Establish masters' programs in business and human resource development within the next three years.
2. Increase by 20 percent the scores achieved by accepted students on their appropriate entrance examinations.
3. Establish and implement a measurable quality indicator program with specific criteria designed to improve teaching effectiveness and faculty scholarship.
4. Develop a comprehensive salary and benefit program that will provide for appropriate salary, equity, health, and retirement incentives for faculty, staff, and administration.

A statement of whether resources will be available cannot be made without at least some analysis of the cost of providing services for activities which must break even. For new programs and initiatives, the expenditures and revenues (which likely include both tuition and contributions) associated with the program should have been analyzed before introduction. For existing programs, contributions can be analyzed to project continued levels of support. This information, combined with estimates of expenses involved in implementing the marketing strategy for recruiting new students and retaining returning students, provides a basis for statements of objectives about contributions.

Sample statements are shown in Exhibit 6.3 as illustrations of contribution objectives. Again, nebulous statements such as "acceptable contribution levels" or "reasonable contributions" should be avoided because of the possible variations in definition and the lack of quantifiability.

In setting objectives, they are first stated in terms of what we want to accomplish, but as we develop the strategy we might discover that we cannot afford what we want. The available resources committed to a given program or service might not be sufficient to achieve a stated objective; if the planning process is resource-controlled, the objectives must be altered. It must be remembered that objectives are not fate, but they are direction. They are not commands, but they become commitments. As a planner, you must not fall into the trap of thinking that once objectives are set they cannot or should not be altered.

Exhibit 6.3. Examples of Financial and Development Objectives

1. Produce net contributions of $2.6 million for the next fiscal year.
2. Generate an 8 percent per year average increase in contributions to the general unrestricted fund for the next five years using the base of $2.6 million.
3. Call every alumni twice during the next year; increase the number of givers by 15 percent and the amount of giving by 20 percent.
4. Hold a major donor event to coincide with announcement of new program initiatives next October; increase attendance to 75 people.

Keep in mind that the interactive processes of setting objectives and developing strategies must be used to set objectives that are realistic. The costs of many aspects of strategy cannot be estimated until a written statement of strategy is developed. If the strategy calls for a new program, for example, that strategy must be spelled out in detail before costs can be estimated (see Chapter 7).

OTHER LONGER-TERM GOALS/OBJECTIVES

The above discussion has focused on three Key Result Areas: Student Objectives, Academic Program Objectives, and Financial and Development Objectives. Exhibit 6.4 provides examples of additional objectives/goals pertinent to an educational institution in the longer run.

Exhibit 6.4. Examples of Institutional Goals/Objectives in the Three-to-Five-Year Time Horizon (Private Higher Education)

1. Establish degree programs at a higher level (such as master's level in a baccalaureate level institution).
2. Establish a quality indicator program with specific criteria designed to improve teaching effectiveness, student entry qualifications, faculty scholarship, instructional resources, and academic support.
3. Establish at least one nontraditional degree program that will be self-sufficient.
4. Achieve placement of graduates in their fields of study at a level commensurate with comparable educational institutions.
5. Receive graduate ratings from employers that are consistently high in terms of potential, competence, and character.
6. Implement a plan to double the institution's endowment within five years.
7. Develop a comprehensive salary and benefit program that will provide for appropriate salary, equity, health, and retirement incentives.
8. Improve the effectiveness of yield in the various stages of the enrollment management process—from student inquiry to application to acceptance to matriculation to graduation and beyond.

USING ENVIRONMENTAL ANALYSIS DATA
TO SET OBJECTIVES

The objectives of a given plan are based on the data provided in the situation analysis discussed earlier. In other words, good objectives are based on a careful analysis of the external and internal environment of a private higher education institution. A specific example of how data are used in setting objectives may help in understanding this point. Consider information in "Key Result Areas" in Appendix A-1 of the "Strategic Planning at Thorndyke College" case study.

The city in which Thorndyke College is located is ripe for a new program initiative. The following facts and perceptions were collected by the strategic planning task force's environmental scan:

1. Enrollment growth rates: Enrollment growth at comparable institutions (located in surrounding communities within 100 miles of the city of Thorndyke) has averaged 5.6 percent/year over the past three years; Thorndyke's average is 6.9 percent overall and a strong 20.9 percent/year in the part-time student category.
2. Tuition and fees: Since 1990 (five years), comparable institutions have averaged tuition and fee increases of 7.7 percent/year, whereas Thorndyke's average annual increase has been 6.7 percent and actual tuition is lower at Thorndyke.
3. Thorndyke former students who did not graduate but live in the area are finding it increasingly more difficult to find employment in jobs for which they were trained. Degree completion programs are designed to address this.

The environmental factors were, for the most part, favorable, and the adult evening student market had a healthy growth rate. Exhibit 6.5 combines environmental analysis data to show the potential for a new degree completion program.

Objectives derived through such a process represent the realities of the area and also the institution's willingness and ability to commit itself to such objectives. This example should also reemphasize the logic in the strategic planning format. The analysis precedes

Exhibit 6.5. Potential for New Degree Completion Program

1. Enrollment growth over past three years at comparable institutions is 5.6 percent/year.
2. Enrollment growth at Thorndyke is 6.9 percent/year total; 20.9 percent/year in part-time students.
3. Tuition increases over past five years are 7.7 percent/year at comparable institutions; 6.7 percent/year at Thorndyke. Adult, fully employed degree completion students can/will likely pay higher tuition rates.
4. A degree completion program in human resource management and leadership development will provide the needed match between perceived students' needs and the curriculum (see case study Appendix A-2, Strategic Planning Issues by Strategic Planning Task Force, item 4).
5. Student outcomes of finding satisfying jobs in their areas of training will be enhanced (see case study Appendix A-2, Strategic Planning Issues by Strategic Planning Task Force, item 2).
6. Objective: Implement a degree completion program with two initial cohorts of 20 students each with a four-year goal of ten cohorts (strategies would include development of a team inside the institution to guide the process, contact with outside organizations to help in the process, and other specific strategies toward implementation).

setting objectives, because objectives must be based on realistic information that only a careful analysis can provide.

CONGRUENT OBJECTIVES AT DIFFERENT INSTITUTIONAL LEVELS

Earlier in this chapter, we alluded to the need for congruence between mission and objectives. Now that objectives have been covered, it is useful to illustrate the congruence factor at differing levels of the institution. Exhibit 6.6 provides examples.

PERFORMANCE CONTRACTS

Objectives can become the basis of a performance contract for administration and staff members (between the individual and the

Exhibit 6.6. Examples of Congruent Goals and Objectives at Different Levels of the Institution

---

I. University/College Goal: Improve the incidence and timeliness of graduate placement in jobs for which students were trained.

  A. School/Department of Education Goal: Increase "action learning" opportunities in the curriculum through internships, mentorships, practicum, and independent study with the intent of enhancing students' resumes and/or opening up the possibilities of staying on in full-time, permanent capacities.

    1. Objective #1: By January (year), establish an advisory board of at least 15 education/community leaders who will provide ideas and resources to help develop an "inventory" of internships, mentorships, practicum, and similar "hands-on" learning opportunities.

    2. Objective #2: By May (year), advisory board to provide a list of action learning opportunities for each graduating senior that will enhance student's marketability to secure a job upon graduation.

  B. School/Department of Business Goal: Admit on-campus and distance education students capable of building dynamic institutions—either as entrepreneurs or as employees capable of moving up the corporate ladder.

    1. Objective #1: By next fall, implement an honors program recruiting from quality feeder high schools and institutions at least 20 students who have high leadership potential as indicated by our new honors admissions criteria.

    2. Objective #2: Ask each corporate executive on the Advisory Board to recommend within 90 days our "fast track" degree program to three other local corporate executives for their companies' up and coming young movers and shakers.

II. University/College Goal: Prepare students through innovative residency and nontraditional (e.g., distance) educational delivery systems to assume leadership positions in the fields of study offered by the institution.

  A. School/Department Goal: Establish and implement a new initiative providing for a bachelor's degree in Organizational Management and/or Leadership Development that will focus on adult learners currently in management/leadership career tracks.

    1. Through traditional and innovative means ensure students have management potential and demonstrate leadership characteristics in the interview/admissions process.

    2. Within five years of graduation, 75 percent of the alumni will have assumed positions of leadership responsibility (i.e., administration, supervision, lobbying, federal or state government positions, faculty teaching/research positions, master's/doctoral candidates, private school leadership, department chairs, or entrepreneurs in other areas).

institution or between individuals). As an example, note how the objectives for a department head can become a performance contract through the following process:

1. Properly written objectives submitted to the dean.
2. Items discussed and negotiated with the dean.
3. Objectives resubmitted to the dean.
4. List approved by both parties (and perhaps the institution's president or even the governing board).
5. In some institutions, both parties sign an objectives sheet.

Exhibit 6.7 provides sample objectives for an administrator.

PERIODIC REVIEW

One practical, easy way to record, communicate, measure, and update objectives is through a "Performance Plan Book" or "Management Plan Book." All objectives for the institution should be in this book. Objectives can be reviewed each quarter/semester and updated. Examples of how objectives might be set up in a management plan book and how they can be listed, kept track of, and presented for review are shown in Exhibits 6.8 and 6.9. This process greatly reduces paperwork and provides a convenient method for review.

SUMMARY

Setting objectives is another major part of the strategic planning process. The necessity for objectives as well as their characteristics was presented here to lay the groundwork for identifying basic types of objectives for such Key Result Areas as student objectives, academic programs, and funding/development functions. The statements of objectives given as examples in this chapter possess the basic characteristics needed to serve both as a source of direction and in evaluation of the strategies developed in the plan.

Exhibit 6.7. Sample Objectives for an Administrator Department: Chair Objectives (Year)

I. Routine Objectives
 1. To make at least one "peer review" faculty teaching assessment per week.
 2. To review each degree program's objectives and accomplishments by January 5, June 5.
 3. To attend the annual regional accreditation meeting.

II. Problem-Solving Objectives
 1. To develop and implement a plan to get the alumni more involved in the affairs of the college by October 31.
 2. To develop staff training seminar on computer literacy by January 31.
 3. To develop a set of criteria and measurable objectives for improving student retention rate.

III. Innovative Objectives
 1. To devise a better system of advising students in time for the start of the (year)-(year) academic year.
 2. To develop a method or methods to give all department heads feedback on their budget performances. At least one method to be implemented by May 1st, and another method implemented by June 1st.

IV. Personal Objectives
 1. To improve my understanding of the latest trends in educational technology; attend one convention and two seminars during the academic year.
 2. To exercise four times per week.

V. Team Objectives
 1. To work with the staff on revision and update of the departmental strategic plan to be presented to the board of trustees in July.
 2. To meet with the staff each Wednesday to troubleshoot problems and coordinate activities.
 3. Be active in working on at least one institution-wide activity each year.

VI. Budget Objectives
 1. To operate within the $100,000 yearly marketing budget.
 2. To retire 10 percent of the debt on the building.

VII. Professional Development Objectives
 1. Read at least one periodical each week.
 2. Complete the reading of at least one book per month.
 3. Deliver at least one major paper this year.
 4. Speak to at least one group every 60 days.
 5. Attend two conventions in teaching/research fields of expertise each year.

VIII. Community Objectives
 1. Continue active involvement in a church/community organization.
 2. Contribute in a meaningful way to at least one annual community event.

Exhibit 6.8. Sample Management Plan Book Overall Objectives, (Year) - (Year)

	(year)	(year)	(year)
STUDENT OBJECTIVES			
Enrollment			
Graduate Placement in Area of Training			
Student Satisfaction with Education			
ACADEMIC PROGRAM			
Faculty: Professional Development Plan Written and Monitored			
Finish Modules Through Degree Completion Program			
Finish Academic Program Through Distance Education			
FINANCIAL (Per Existing Program)			
Average Donations			
New Donors/Sponsors			
Budget			
Current Ratio			
Fixed Asset Turnover/Donations/Net Fixed Assets			
Total Asset Turnover/Donations/Total Assets			
Debt Ratio/Total Debt/Total Assets			
Debt/Total Funding			
Times Interest Earned/Donations/Interest			
STAFF			
Administration			
Staff			
Consultants			
BUILDINGS			
Build/Buy/Rent a New Facility			
Existing Facilities Improvement			
New Equipment			
Equipment Repair or Replacement			
EXISTING FACILITIES			
Systematic Safety Check			
Heating and Cooling			
Security: Burglar Alarms			
Lighting			
Parking			
Sound System/Other Special Systems			
STAFF/VOLUNTEER TRAINING AND MORALE			
Administration In-Service Seminars			
Staff Training: In-House			
Staff Training: External Seminars			
Yearly Attitude Survey			
PUBLIC RESPONSIBILITY			
Cooperative Funding Efforts with Other Institutions			
Facilities Sharing			

Exhibit 6.8 (continued)

	(year)	(year)	(year)
NEW PROGRAMS (Per Program)			
Clientele Need Assessment			
Competing Programs			
Funding Sources			
Funding Levels			
Curriculum/Course/Module			
Development			
Development/Start-Up Expenses			
Operating Budgets			
Staff Required			
Faculty Staffing			
SUPPORT HARDWARE/SOFTWARE			
Hardware Adequacy			
Software Adequacy			
Hardware/Software Planning Awareness			
of Forthcoming Technological Change			
Staff			
Space			
Accomplished Outcomes			

Exhibit 6.9. Sample Review Sheet Management Plan, (Year)

Objectives	Results
I. Routine: Department chair will meet every report deadline outlined in the Chair's Manual each calendar quarter in (year).	On target
II. Budget Performance: Operate within the $450,000 department budget throughout fiscal (year).	On target
III. Problem Solving: Develop a set of criteria for admitting students in the new degree program by March 31, (year).	Met 90%
Team IV. Social Science chair will work with the head of admissions to develop a faster way to handle enrollment inquiries, checking out by April (year) software cost and effectiveness.	50% done
V. Innovative: Devise a better system of screening prospective faculty members by February (year).	Done
VI. Personal: Read the book, *Strategic Planning for Private Higher Education*; attend communication course, fall of (year)	Book completed; course registration mailed

OBJECTIVES WORKSHEET

This worksheet will aid in developing and testing objectives for a private higher education institution.

I. Developing Objectives

A. Answer these questions first:

1. What do the institution's objectives need to relate to–students, faculty/staff, academic programs, funding, or all four? What about other Key Result Areas?

   - _____

   _____

   - _____

   _____

   - _____

   _____

   - _____

   _____

2. What needs to happen for the institution's programs to be successful? In other words, how many people need to enroll, graduate, publish, obtain grants, contribute, obtain employment, etc.? When do you want these things to happen (give specific date)?

   - _____

   _____

   - _____

   _____

- _____

  _____

- _____

  _____

B. Now write your objectives. Use the information in your answers above to write statements of your objectives for each Key Result Area.

   1. Key Result Area No. 1:_____

   Objective 1:_____

  _____

  _____

   Objective 2:_____

  _____

  _____

   Objective 3:_____

  _____

  _____

   (Duplicate for each Key Result Area.)

II. Testing Objectives

A. Now test each statement made above using the following criteria:

Is each statement relevant to the basic purpose of your institution?

   1._____

   2._____

   3._____

Is each statement practical?

1._____

2._____

3._____

Does each statement provide a challenge?

1._____

2._____

3._____

Is each stated in objectively measurable terms?

1._____

2._____

3._____

Do you have a specific date for completion?

1._____

2._____

3._____

Does each statement contribute to a balance of activities in line with your institution's strengths and weaknesses?

1._____

2._____

3._____

B. Now test the goal-setting process in the institution:

1. Is there a clear process of setting goals and objectives?

_____

_____

_____

2. What are the goals and objectives for your institution for the current planning year?

_____

_____

_____

3. Is there clear evidence that goals and objectives are written at the institutional level and at the school/college/department level?

_____

_____

_____

4. Do institution-wide level goals and objectives have a clear relationship to vision/mission/purpose?

_____

_____

_____

Chapter 7

Developing Strategy and Action Plans

Strategy making and strategy implementation requires key leadership skills such as: fostering ownership in vision, mission, values of the institution, building people relationships based on trust, developing a culture consistent with vision/mission.

–George Keller

If we can know where we are and something about how we got there, we might see where we are treading—and if the outcomes which lie naturally in our course are unacceptable, to make timely change.

–Abraham Lincoln

Just being able to conceive bold new strategies is not enough. The general manager must also be able to translate his or her strategic vision into concrete steps that "get things done."

–Richard G. Hamermesh

After developing a set of objectives for the time period covered by the strategic plan, the strategy necessary for accomplishing those objectives must be formulated. First, an overall strategy must be designed. Then the operating details of that strategy as it relates to providing services, promoting operations, determining location, and enlisting funding support must be planned to guide the institution's efforts. This chapter introduces the concept of strategy;

describes strategy elements; explains approaches to strategy development; and provides details for strategy implementation (also called action plans).

STRATEGY CONCEPTS

The word "strategy" has been used in a number of ways over the years and especially so in the context of business. Often, it is confused with the terms "objective," "policy," "procedure," and "tactic." Strategy may be defined as the course of action(s) taken by an institution to achieve its objectives. It is the catalyst or dynamic element of administration which enables the institution to accomplish its objectives. Meyer's (1991) research indicates another characteristic of strategy: it brings together the theoretical and the practical, the power of the conceptual with the applied processes of planning.

Strategic Thinking

Strategy making is the thinking stage of strategic planning. Strategic thinking is akin to critical thinking, a familiar concept in education. Traditionally, critical thinking has been identified with the field of logic and the mental ability to reason in the abstract. Today, critical thinking is an essential element of most disciplines including management, leadership, and strategic planning. Strategic thinking might be explained as focusing on higher level learning and more complex thinking abilities. It is often involved with relating seemingly diverse elements of the institution and its environment.

A leader who thinks strategically will tend to focus on the following activities:

- Asking and seeking answers to penetrating questions which affect survival of the institution
- Scanning the external environment and the internal culture for unique ways of "doing more with less at higher quality"
- Conceptualizing direction-setting actions for the institution
- Identifying areas of change that will impact the vision, mission, and overall goals of the institution

- Looking at the big picture–across traditional boundaries and beyond the next two to three years
- Emphasizing the why and the how (instead of what) of strategy design and implementation
- Searching for the best competitive advantage, or best competitive position relative to other key institutions, which may target similar student markets and donors

Strategic thinking emphasizes development and implementation of institution-wide or overall strategies with accountability toward effectiveness, efficiency, and quality in mind.

Strategy development is both a science and an art and is a product of both logic and creativity. The scientific aspect deals with assembling and allocating the resources necessary to achieve an institution's objectives with emphasis on opportunities, costs, and time. The art of strategy making is mainly concerned with the utilization of resources including motivation of the people, sensitivity to the environment, and ability to adapt to changing conditions.

Only a small percentage of institutions in private higher education have endowments that produce income sufficient to contribute more that 5 to 10 percent of the annual operating budget. Thus, most of private higher education receives 90 percent or more of their current fund revenues in the forms of student tuition, fees, and current fund gift income. Add to this characteristic the fact that tuition at private institutions is higher than comparable public institutions competing in the same geographic market. Faced with such a set of market conditions where price competition (tuition) is out of the picture, private institutions must pay close attention to marketing strategy and techniques as well as to uniqueness of academic programs in order to achieve their missions and survive. Strategies must be developed to achieve goals in the areas of tuition/fees (student market) and gift income (contributors). Thus, the roles of both student and donor as customers form the starting point for the development of strategy. An additional stakeholder has become increasingly important in this context–employers of the institution's graduates. In a presentation at a convention sponsored by the Council for Adult and Experential Learning, Dean Scott S. Cowen (1995) of the Weatherhead School of Business at Case Western Reserve University stated that these "are the most important stakeholders."

The Concept of Positioning

Positioning an institution is answering the question: "How do we distinguish ourselves from other higher education institutions in the marketplace?" Thus, we might assess the competitive forces operating in the external environment and "position" our institution in a context and in a direction that we may achieve mission and goals on a sustained basis, while minimizing the pulling power of other educational institutions upon our targeted stakeholders, especially students and contributors. Stevens, Loudon, and Warren (1991) explain positioning in the context of strategy development as linking the organization's distinctive competencies (what the institution does well) with customers' needs (student learning and gainful employment).

The outcome of effective strategy making and implementation is to "position" the institution is such a way that it has improved probability of achieving its mission, goals, and objectives at or above acceptable levels of quality. For private higher education, Wallingford and Berger explain the value of strategy well—"it is the combination of target market, programs, institutional policies and other factors that create a unique positioning of the institution. More specifically, the course offerings and programs of the institution need to be carefully selected and developed in terms of the positioning which the institution has selected for itself in the marketplace. This focus will serve to build enrollment, retention and loyalty" (Wallingford and Berger, 1993).

Positioning or repositioning an institution is often driven by changes in the external environment over which the administration has no control. When enrollments are dropping and/or competition is increasing for shrinking pools of students, institutions must apply better marketing strategies in strategic planning to improve the chances of long-term survival (Wallingford and Berger, 1993).

PREMARKETING STRATEGIES

One area of operations that has received increasing attention in recent years is the use of marketing in institutions of higher learning. Prior to developing specific marketing strategies aimed at specific market segments and using specific marketing programs, there is a need to consider broader market opportunities and strategies which precede the selection of the more detailed marketing strategy used in a specific action plan.

Since most institutions have growth as one of their basic objectives, one area of strategy development revolves around the question of how growth will be obtained. There are three possible alternative growth strategies:

1. Product/Market Expansion Strategies
2. Integrative Strategies
3. Diversification Strategies

These strategic alternatives can be illustrated in a 2×2 matrix called a product/market growth matrix. This type of matrix is illustrated in Exhibit 7.1.[1]

Exhibit 7.1. Product/Market Matrix

	EXISTING SERVICE	NEW SERVICE
EXISTING MARKET	MARKET PENETRATION	PRODUCT DEVELOPMENT
NEW MARKET	MARKET DEVELOPMENT	DIVERSIFICATION

Product/Market Expansion Strategies

Product/market expansion strategies involve growth through expansion of existing product markets, development of new products aimed at existing markets, or development of new markets for existing products. Each of these strategic options carries with it advantages and risks as far as the administration is concerned. In a market penetration strategy, the administration has the advantage of both product knowledge and existing markets. The obvious disadvantage is the fact that the products will eventually pass through various product life-cycle stages ending with sales decline and extinction.

In a product development strategy, the advantage the administration has is in knowledge of the market they are dealing with since the products are aimed at existing markets. The disadvantage is lack of product knowledge.

When a market development strategy is used, product knowledge is the advantage, while a lack of market knowledge is the disadvantage. When a diversification strategy is used, the administration is under the most strain. They have neither product knowledge nor market knowledge as an advantage, so they must quickly acquire this knowledge, or rely on acquiring people who already possess product/market knowledge, in this specific area, or use consultants with this knowledge/experience.

Market penetration is a strategy that involves growth through increasing use of existing products in existing markets. This expansion of sales can come about by (1) altering purchase patterns of existing students–getting them to take more classes when they enroll or to enroll in additional semesters, such as summer school; (2) attracting nonstudents to enroll; and (3) attracting students from other institutions to switch, thereby increasing market share. Alternatives 1 and 2 involve increasing the total size of the market, while alternative 3 involves increasing market share.

Product development is a strategy for increasing Student Credit Hours (SCHs) through the introduction of new products to existing markets. Product development involves altering existing products by (1) offering new courses or programs or adding new features, such as a co-op program or a degree completion program; (2) offering different quality levels, such as an executive MBA program; or (3) offering different variations of the existing programs, such as short courses or evening courses.

Market development is a strategy which entails offering existing products to new markets. These markets can be (1) new geographical markets, such as an off-campus site, or branch operations in other areas or in foreign countries, or (2) new market segments not currently using the products, such as programs offered at military bases or large companies within close proximity to the institution.

Integrative Strategies

An institution can choose to grow through integration of activities within its current industry. There are three alternatives for this type of growth: (1) forward integration, (2) backward integration, and (3) horizontal integration:

Forward integration as a growth strategy means the institution looks at the end user—the employers. For example, an institution might consider taking over specific training programs of area companies, such as supervisory management training programs or computer literacy programs.

Backward integration seeks growth through networking with institutions who are suppliers—high schools or community colleges. For example, a college might develop a "young executives" program aimed at high school students considering careers in business, or offering college-level courses at local high schools for seniors or advanced students.

Horizontal integration seeks growth through networking with sister institutions or taking over programs "abandoned" by other institutions. This strategy may involve developing joint programs with other institutions, such as offering programs at institutions in foreign countries where teaching and administrative activities are shared by the institutions involved.

Diversification Strategies

A final strategic alternative for growth is through diversification. Diversification entails introducing new products into new markets or merging with other institutions which are already in these new product/market situations. Diversification strategies can take various forms. The most common are (1) product/technology-related, (2) market-related, and (3) nonproduct/nonmarket-related.

Product/technology diversification consists of adding services that are technologically related to existing products even though they are aimed at different markets. For example, an institution that has a medical technology program might train lab technicians in local labs on the latest equipment or procedures used in laboratory testing.

Market-related diversification consists of introducing services aimed at the same market even though the product technologies are different. For example, offering courses through interactive television to nontraditional students or in distance learning programs.

Nonproduct/nonmarket-related diversification, sometimes called conglomerate diversification, seeks to add new services aimed at new classes of customers. An example would be developing an "English Language Institute" on campus to teach English to foreign students who are coming to U.S. institutions, or to foreigners who want to learn English for some other reasons.

Strategy Selection Alternatives

Each of the growth strategies described above provides alternatives for an institution seeking growth. While each type has been treated as a separate strategic alternative, it is possible to pursue more than one strategy at the same time, given the administrative and financial resources needed for such growth.

STRATEGIES FOR EXISTING
STRATEGIC PLANNING UNITS

The Boston Consulting Group, a well-known consulting organization, has developed an approach to strategic planning which permits classifying each strategic unit, or strategic planning unit, (SPU) on the basis of its relative market share and growth potential.[2] This approach, depicted in Exhibit 7.2, permits development of strategies for each SPU based on its classification within the matrix. Within an educational context, this normally involves programs, divisions, or schools/colleges within the university.

The vertical axis shows annualized-market growth rates for each SPU in its respective market. The division of high-low rates at 10 percent is arbitrary.

Exhibit 7.2. Boston Consulting Group Matrix: Relative Market Share

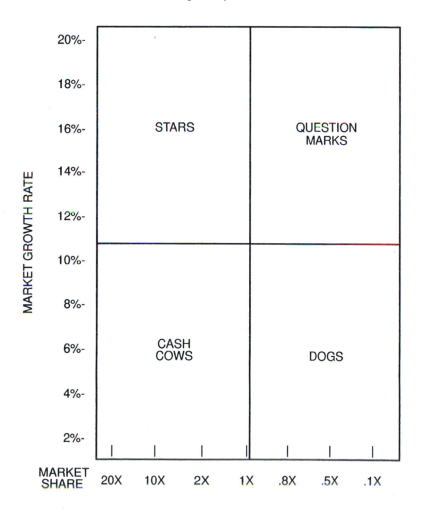

The horizontal axis shows the market share of each SPU in relation to the industry leaders. Thus, it is relative market share and not absolute market share. If relative market share for an SPU is $1.5\times$, this means that the SPU is the market leader and its share is one-and-a-half times greater than the next closest competitor. A relative market share of $.8\times$ would indicate that the SPU's market share is 80 percent of the market leader's share. Relative market shares put each SPU in relation to the leader and provide more information about market position than would absolute market share. The $1.5\times$ division is again an arbitrary point for separating SPUs into high-low relative market shares.

Given this information, each SPU is placed in one of four quadrants resulting in the following four classifications of SPUs:

1. *Cash Cows*–A cash cow is an SPU with a high relative market share compared to other institutions in the market, but it is in an educational area that has a low annual growth rate. These SPUs generate more than enough cash to cover operating expenses but their growth rates do not warrant large investments in those programs. The cash generated can therefore be used to support other SPUs which offer more potential for growth. In recent years, business programs usually fall into this quadrant.
2. *Stars*–Stars are those SPUs which have a high relative market share and are also in industries with expected high rates of growth. Their high growth rates usually represent high demand for cash to finance their growth. Medical-related programs such as pharmacy or occupational therapy could be current examples of such SPUs.
3. *Question Marks*–Question marks are those SPUs which have a low relative market share but are in industries which have a high annual rate of growth. The potential exists for them to become stars, but their low relative share represents a major challenge to create strategies capable of increasing relative market share. A physical or occupational therapy program with low enrollment would be an example of this type of SPU.
4. *Dogs*–Dogs are SPUs which not only have low relative market share but also are in industries which have low-growth poten-

tial. They might not be operating at a loss but they generate only enough cash to maintain their operations and market share.

Classifying an institution's SPUs into such a matrix helps define the current position of each SPU and also suggests strategic options for the administration to improve performance of existing programs. While the position of an SPU will change over time because of changes in growth rates or market position, the following strategic actions are implied for the four cells:

1. *"Milk" Cows*–The strategy for these cash cows is to spend enough on them to maintain their market shares ("keep them healthy") so they can continue to generate SCHs.
2. *"Shine" Stars*–The strategy for these stars is to continue to invest funds into these SPUs to support their growth rate and high market shares. They will eventually slow in growth and become cash cows themselves and help generate funds for new stars.
3. *"Answer" Questions*–The strategy for these SPUs would involve one of two options: develop and test strategies for improving market share; or phase out of these SPUs and use the funds saved for supporting other more promising SPUs.
4. *"Eliminate" Dogs*–These SPUs with the low-share, low-growth potential are prime prospects for phase out. Expenditures saved by phasing out these SPUs can be reinvested in other SPUs with more potential.

MARKET SEGMENTATION

Nothing is more central to marketing than consumer analysis. This section focuses on consumers' needs which are the pivotal point around which objectives and strategies are developed. The key words in this section are "consumer" and "analysis." The objective of the process is understanding consumers' needs–which is accomplished through analysis. The word "analysis" simply means to break into parts. The tools used in this analysis activity comprise the primary focus of this chapter.

Selecting the appropriate segments and successfully attracting customers is the basis for an organization's survival and growth. Once a specific market segment has been identified, its size must be estimated. This estimate becomes a key to assessing the attractiveness of the segment.

One fundamental concept that underlies market analysis is what is sometimes referred to as a "market" but is actually a composite of smaller markets, each with identifiable characteristics. When we speak of the student market, for example, we are making reference to a large market which is composed of smaller submarkets or segments. This market can be segmented in several ways to identify the various submarkets. The age of the students, for example, may be used to identify at least two submarkets or segments: traditional and nontraditional. This process of breaking up a market into smaller parts or segments is usually referred to as market segmentation. The basic premise is that the needs of consumers in one segment are different from those in another segment and, therefore, different marketing strategies should be used to reach different segments. The results of the analysis should be an understanding of consumers' needs by segment and some insight into the types of strategies needed to meet those needs. This is the basis of the entire planning process if a consumer-oriented approach is to be used in planning.

For each segment that is identified, two basic questions must be asked: (1) What are the identifying characteristics of that segment? and (2) What is its size? Answering the first question helps define consumers' needs and helps develop a profile of consumers for each segment–the qualitative side of the market. The answer to the second question provides information on the size or the quantitative side of the market.

Once the segments are identified, the organization must decide toward which ones they want to direct their marketing effort. This process is referred to as target marketing. It involves directing marketing efforts at specific identifiable market segments which have been selected because of their size and characteristics.

Basis for Market Segmentation

There are several commonly used categories for market segmentation. These include geographic, demographic, usage, benefits sought, stage in the family life cycle, and psychographics. These may be combined to provide a more thorough understanding of a market segment.

Geographic and Demographic Segmentation

The most commonly used bases for segmentation utilize geographic and demographic variables. Geographic segmentation involves use of geographic areas such as county, state, regional, and national as the basis of segmentation. For many organizations, this is a logical framework because of differences between areas. They may offer their services in a few areas and not do anything in others. They are using geographic location to segment the customers they will serve.

Demographic segmentation uses variables such as sex, age, income, marital status, race, and educational level as the bases for segmenting a market. These variables are appropriate for many types of educational services. For example, to reach older students who already have careers, evening or weekend courses might be offered to meet the needs of this group.

Segmentation by Service Usage

Another approach to market segmentation concentrates on the product usage patterns of consumers. Consumers are classified as users or nonusers, and users are further classified as light, medium, and heavy users. In many service categories, a small percentage of the consumers account for a majority of the purchasers. In an educational setting we commonly use full-time or part-time as terms to differentiate these user groups.

Benefit Segmentation

Another way to segment markets is based on the benefits the buyers expect to receive upon purchase or use of a service. For example, educational organizations can create separate educational tracks for students who are degree seeking and those who just want the information offered in a few selected courses. Some institutions set up complete programs aimed at the nondegree-seeking segment when the size of this segment justifies such actions.

Segmentation by Family Life-Cycle Stage

The *family life cycle* is the process of family formation and dissolution. Using this concept, the marketer combines the family characteristics of age, marital status, and presence and ages of children to develop programs and services aimed at various segments.

A five-stage family life cycle with several subcategories has been proposed. These stages are shown in Exhibit 7.3.

The characteristics and needs of people in each life-cycle stage often vary considerably with people in other stages. Young singles have relatively few financial burdens, and are recreation-oriented. By contrast, young marrieds with young children tend to have low liquid assets, and they are more likely to watch television than young singles or young marrieds without children. The empty-nest

Exhibit 7.3. Family Life-Cycle Stages

1. Young Single (under 35)
2. Young Married without Children (under 35)
3. Other Young (under 35)
   a. Young Divorced without Children
   b. Young Married with Children
   c. Young Divorced with Children
4. Middle-Aged (35-64)
   a. Single
   b. Middle-Aged Married without Children
   c. Middle-Aged Divorced without Children
   d. Middle-Aged Married with Children
   e. Middle-Aged Divorced with Children
   f. Middle-Aged Married without Dependent Children
   g. Middle-Aged Divorced without Dependent Children
5. Older (65 and older)
   a. Older Married
   b. Older Unmarried (Divorced, Widowed, Single)
6. Other
   All Adults and Children not Accounted for by Family Life-Cycle Stages

households include those in the middle-age and older categories with no dependent children and who are more likely to have more disposable income; more time for recreation, self-education, and travel; and have more than one member in the labor force, in comparison with their full-nest counterparts with younger children. Similar differences are evident in the other stages of the family life cycle.

Analysis of life-cycle stages often gives better results than reliance on single variables, such as age. The family of four, headed by parents in their twenties, usually has a different pattern of expenditures than a single person of the same age.

Many individuals make career changes when they become empty-nesters. These career changes often require these individuals to "retool" for their new careers through educational activities aimed at preparing them for these sometimes dramatic changes in occupations. This creates opportunities for educational service providers to create programs for these individuals, such as offering specialized programs aimed at specific career changes. Real estate courses, insurance courses, and computer courses offered to these students is an example of how this segmentation approach can lead to altering programs in response to a specific segment's needs.

PSYCHOGRAPHICS/LIFESTYLE SEGMENTATION

Demographic characteristics lack "richness" in describing consumers for market segmentation and strategy development. Consequently, many organizations have found lifestyle and psychographic segmentation to be a better way to define markets. Lifestyle refers to a person's unique pattern of living which influences and is reflected by his or her consumption behavior. *Psychographics* has to do with mental profiles of consumers; it allows the marketer to define consumers' lifestyles in measurable terms. And by incorporating lifestyle characteristics, in addition to demographics, marketers obtain a better, more true-to-life portrait of target consumers.

Lifestyle-segmentation research examines (1) *Activities* consumers engage in, e.g., work, hobbies, social events, vacations, entertainment, and shopping; (2) *Interests* they have in such subjects as family, home, job, and community, for example; and (3) *Opinions* or views they hold about themselves and the world around them, including such things as social issues, politics, business, products, economics, culture, and the future. These three topics on which information is gathered in a lifestyle segmentation study are referred to simply as *AIOs*.

Armed with AIOs, demographics, and the data such as product and media usage, the marketer can construct user profits. The analysis involves relating levels of agreement/disagreement with perhaps 300 AIO statements in a questionnaire (e.g., "I like gardening," "I enjoy going to concerts," "There should be a gun in every house," "I stay home most evenings," and "There is a lot of love in our family") with demographic characteristics, product usage, and media exposure. Typically, a pattern emerges in which AIO statements cluster together, meaning that similar respondents are grouped together on a lifestyle basis. The marketer then must determine which lifestyle segment is desirable as a target group and how best to appeal to them with the marketing mix.

Target Marketing

While the analysis of market segments leads to an understanding of the size and nature of each segment which could be served, decisions must be made about which segments will be served. This decision-making process is usually referred to as target marketing.

Target marketing moves the marketing strategy development process from analysis to action. Decisions must be made about which market segments will be targeted for marketing effort, what positioning strategy will be used, and the exact nature of the services to be offered (fees/tuition, promotion, and where the services will be offered).

As is shown in Exhibit 7.4, there is a logical flow in the strategy development process from raising questions about the size and nature of various segments (market segmentation) to the selection of specific segments to target for marketing effort (target marketing). Analysis of the segments precedes the selection of segments to target with marketing effort. Therefore, we select only those segments we have analyzed and have decided represent the best opportunity for our efforts.

We end the process by developing the specific marketing mix we want to use to go after specific market segments. If the needs of the

Exhibit 7.4. Marketing Strategy Development Process

MARKET SEGMENTATION	TARGET MARKETING
1. What segments exist in the market?	4. Which specific segments do we want to target?
2. What are their sizes and characteristics?	5. How should we position ourselves in these segments?
3. Which ones offer the most opportunity?	6. What should our marketing strategies be for these segments?

segments differ, then we must develop several marketing mixes, each designed to meet the needs of those in a particular segment.

FACTORS INFLUENCING THE STRATEGY SELECTED

At least four factors influence the choice of a strategy selected by the institution: its internal resources, the distinctive competencies of leaders and members, the stage in the institution's life cycle, and strategies used by other institutions. There is no one best strategy which will always prove successful. Instead, the strategy that is chosen must be the one that is best for the institution, given the nature of these four factors. Resources, for example, might limit the institution to a focus strategy. The institution might even be an innovator in terms of ideas but not have the financial, communications, or personnel resources to offer other services.

As emphasized in Chapter 3, a private higher education institution's strategy must be derived from its institutional mission and objectives. If the institutional mission is focused on serving needs of diverse groups, then the strategy used must be one that is compatible. In other words, what an institution *does* must be congruent with what it *is*.

The distinctive competencies of the educational institution have a direct bearing on the strategy selected. Distinctive skills and experience in dealing with the physically challenged, for example, can influence strategy choice. These distinctive competencies are the basis of doing things well.

The institution's life-cycle stage is an additional factor influencing strategy selection. For example, an institution may begin with a focus strategy but add programs over time which serve more varied needs. Repositioning the institution through introducing new programs or serving new markets could be a pivotal point of the strategy.

The strategy selected must be given sufficient time to be implemented and to affect the groups served, but an obviously ineffective strategy should be changed. This concept should be understood without mention, but the resistance to change is a common phenomenon in many institutions.

EXAMPLES OF DIFFERENTIATION AND FOCUS STRATEGIES

Differentiation Strategy at North Central College

A differentiation strategy concentrates on developing and delivering educational services which stand out in the student's mind as distinct from other educational institutions' services. Higher education institutions that employ this strategy seek to meet a broad spectrum of student needs.

North Central College (NCC) is a small liberal arts college located in Naperville, the western suburbs of the Chicago metropolitan region. This private higher education institution exemplifies the use of differentiated strategy. The following illustrates the differentiation:

Traditional Undergraduate Liberal Arts Program
Although demographic studies show traditional-age college students decreasing in numbers, this market segment is still a significant part of NCC's differentiation strategy.

The Center for Continuing Education
NCC administrators recognized the trend toward lifelong learning: a growing market of adult learners who were not necessarily interested in earning a degree as in pursuing knowledge and skills to meet a specific need.

The Evening College

Recognized the needs of a growing market of students who work full-time during the day but wish to finish their degrees in the evening.

The Graduate Program: Selected Master Level Degree Programs

Started with a master's degree program in computer science, expanded to masters' degree programs in business administration and management information systems.

The Weekend College

Another market segment of adult learners prefer concentrated amounts of coursework on weekends rather than several evenings a week. Many of these take the form of degree completion programs with modules (courses) between four and six weeks in length; ability to enter as a junior; and complete the degree in as little as 15 to 22 months (depending upon the major and whether general education requirements [GER] and total hours for graduation are met prior to entry).

Focus Strategy at Regis College

The other basic approach an educational institution can use to pursue its objectives is a focus strategy. A focus strategy concentrates on a single service or category of very similar services which meet the needs of a specific student or donor market. Regis College in Denver, Colorado, uses this strategy. Today, the college offers a wide variety of educational programs to meet needs of a wide variety of students. Regis College is an example of success in applying strategic planning to a private institution at risk of survival:

Regis College in 1980:

- campus of crumbling buildings
- 1,000 students, mostly younger and dependent on some form of government-based student financial aid
- multiple years of deficit spending in the operating fund
- primarily tuition-driven

Regis University (same institution) in 1995:

- 8,000 students, including many adult students employed full-time and taking evening and weekend courses
- annual operating fund with excess revenues over expenditures
- less tuition-driven; student body more diverse in many ways, including less dependence on government student financial aid

Regis College Strategies:

- targeting a new customer segment–adult learners
- improving student service, including simplified registration procedures
- better service and availability of textbooks

The "focus" is understood in emphasizing excellent service in meeting the needs of one market segment–the adult learner. The main advantages of this strategy are (1) it capitalizes on the distinctive competencies of the people involved, and (2) it concentrates on doing one thing well. These advantages can also create a knowledge base of how to carry out certain types of programs, as well as improved efficiency in performing the services.

Implementing Differentiation and Focus Strategies

The above examples of differentiation strategy (North Central College) and focus strategy (Regis College) both required the prerequisite of environmental analysis concerning the fit between the educational services offered (internal core competencies) and the needs of the student market. In the context of the student as customer, an analysis of what an institution of higher education may offer students includes the following:

- Course offerings/programs/degrees
- Admissions procedures
- Target market identification
- Cocurricular activities (athletics, social events, social institutions, etc.)
- Course scheduling

- Counseling (financial, personal, academic)
- Registration and transfer credit evaluation
- Career planning and co-op opportunities
- Cafeteria service
- Parking and housing
- Security

All planning units of the institution (schools; departments; academic support units such as library or computer services; administrative support such as registrar, business office, student services) must be tuned into serving this important stakeholder–the student or prospective student.

Perceived high standards of high quality and exceptional value of the *services* in the mind of the customer, especially the quality of teaching (teachers/faculty are a key success factor), are essential for the private higher education institution (which usually has a price disadvantage) to effectively compete for students in the marketplace.

Notice a characteristic of these basic overall strategies: *matching internal strengths with external opportunities.*

STRATEGIES TO IMPROVE SERVICE EFFECTIVENESS BY SERVICE FACTOR

Exhibit 7.5 provides some examples of linking specific strategy ideas with services that an institution in private higher education might offer.

Of course, the reason behind designing specific strategies for specific customer types is to increase the distinctive image of the institution and thus heighten the perceived differentiation from public and other private higher education institutions.

ACTION (OR OPERATIONAL) PLANS

After all the steps have been taken and a strategy has been developed to meet your objectives and goals, it is time to develop an action (operational) plan. The action plan is the "doing" stage.

Exhibit 7.5. Specific Strategy Ideas Linked with Services

SERVICE FACTOR	SPECIFIC STRATEGY IDEAS
Course Offerings/Programs	Outreach to foreign students (adds element of culture).
Degrees	Honors programs Special scholarships
Admissions	Understand and meet needs of targeted students as they perceive their needs.
Target Market Identification	Nontraditional students with preschool dependents who might need child care.
Cocurricular Activities	Certain potential students will note the quality and quantity of facilities supporting athletics, social institutions, and social events. How well these activities and related facilities match with the student's perceived needs will impact enrollment decisions.
Registration	Registration by mail, by telephone, by e-mail appeal to most students when confronted with the traditional bureaucratic, time-consuming procedures.
Career Planning/Placement	Some students/employers perceive internships, co-op opportunities, and career counseling as important factors in their decisions to enroll.

Here you hire, fire, build, advertise, and so on. How many times has a group of people planned something, become enthusiastic, and nothing happened? This is usually because they did not complete an action plan to implement their strategy.

Action plans need to be developed in all the areas that are used to support the overall strategy. Action plans include the Key Result Areas discussed in Chapter 6. In addition, action plans should include operations, communications, finances/costs, and staffing (accountability). Each of these more detailed plans is designed to spell out what needs to happen in a given area to implement the strategic plan.

The operations plan identifies exactly what services will be provided to a specific group (students, faculty, contributors, alumni, etc.) and the exact nature of these services. For example, if a private higher education institution is trying to launch a new degree program in human resource management to meet needs of adult learners working full-time, program delivery could take many forms. It could be:

- an evening program on campus or at key locations, such as in the downtown area;
- a weekend program on campus or in another nearby town;
- a concentrated two-week residency with assignments due throughout the semester;
- a degree completion program using modular courses operating on a year-round basis starting at different times of the year; or
- a distance education system via computer, Internet, some aspect of correspondence, conference telephone calls, etc.

Each of these, of course, might require different types of faculty, and different locations with varying quality and quantity of learning resources, equipment, and furniture. The communications plan is used to communicate the nature of the program, location, and time to the intended class of students and also to the rest of the institution's membership. This plan also needs to be well thought out and carefully analyzed to avoid a lack of communication or miscommunication.

For example, in developing its action plans, a degree completion program for full-time working adults would need a communications strategy to provide information to prospective students about its user-friendly features. Its communications strategy could involve three key elements—informing, persuading, and reminding:

1. Informing—This involves providing information to individuals and groups about the institution and this new initiative. Specific elements of this plan call for:

    a. Use of videocassette presentations
    b. Newsletters, pamphlets
    c. Personal speaking appearances by administration, and testimonials from friends of the institution who have suc-

cessfully completed a degree completion program at another college

d. Hosting luncheons/dinners sponsored by the institution

e. On-site visits by individuals/groups to the main campus or regional service centers

2. Persuading–This involves presenting the opportunities for earning a degree while keeping a current job, principles for supporting students who might feel uncomfortable having been out of school for several years, and how the educational institution's services fulfill these principles.

   a. Prepare application forms with which service recipients may request additional information or interested individuals may apply as volunteers.

   b. Provide convenient means for individuals to offer financial support or volunteer their time and services.

3. Reminding–This aspect of the strategy is to continue to provide information to people already familiar with the institution and its innovative degree completion program so they will be constantly reminded of its work and needs.

   a. Send letters/newsletters and other materials regularly.

   b. Provide opportunities for volunteers to write to supporters and future volunteers on a periodic basis.

   c. Develop a complete file of individuals and institutions by name for future mailings.

The staffing plan identifies who will carry out the activities involved. Will it be the institution's paid staff, a consultant, or volunteers? If paid staff are to be used, will they be full-time staff or part-time? If a consultant is used, a contractual agreement must be made as to responsibilities, results, and costs. Of course, if volunteers are to be used, they must be recruited, trained, and supervised. Since many private higher education institutions must rely on nonprofessionals to carry out plans, it might be advisable to develop a recruitment plan just to staff the activity.

Finances must also be planned. This is usually done in the form of a financial budget. The budget is the means to execute the plan. If the financial means to support the plan are not available, you must adjust the objectives. There is a constant interplay between the budget and the plan.

Many people do not understand the budgeting process. The budget is a "tool." Too often, however, the budget becomes the tail wagging the dog for the institution. "We budgeted it so we should spend it," or "We should add a little to this year's budget" are statements that reflect this misunderstanding. Budget money must be tied directly to performance. Performance is measured against objectives. Key Result Areas and objectives in a private higher education institution's operations need to be prioritized. Money and other resources are then allocated.

An example of this interplay can be reflected in the following hypothetical give-and-take regarding the startup of a distance education program in a school of business. In a planning meeting, the dean confronts the realization that most of their resources to support the off-campus component would have to come from incremental revenues generated by the program. The faculty were given a plan whereby salaries could be increased, but no new faculty would be hired for the increased load. As part of the negotiation, faculty also received state-of-the-art computer equipment and were able to delegate a major part of student advising to a qualified full-time recent graduate. In return, commitments were made to move up the learning curve in delivering distance education, and to maintain or exceed accreditation standards of comparability between the two programs—existing on-campus and new off-campus. As a result, the timing for expansion and growth for the program occurred earlier than the financial budget would have allowed.

Shown in the exhibits below are action plans for launching initiatives to counteract enrollment declines and financial problems: for a degree completion program for a private college (Exhibit 7.6), and for financing/development for a private K-12 academy (Exhibit 7.7). The action plans in these examples are related directly to the strategies to be used and the objectives to be accomplished in a step-by-step fashion. This forces planners to align Key Result Areas, objectives, strategies, and action plans together.

Never go into action until the Key Result Areas and corresponding objectives are clear and understood by everyone. It is important

Exhibit 7.6. Action Plan for College Degree Completion Program

KEY RESULT AREA: Increase the enrollment of adult learners in the institution.
OBJECTIVE: To enroll four cohorts of 25 adult learners each in a degree completion program within five months.
STRATEGIES:
    A. Develop a marketing plan for approval by Board of Trustees
    B. Develop complete faculty recruitment and training program
    C. Develop student recruitment plan

ACTION PLAN (partial list)	PERSON RESPONSIBLE	START DATE	DATE COMPLETED
Hire a degree completion consultant			
Develop systems plan for implementation			
Hire a Director			
Identify pool of faculty			
Implement advertising and marketing plans			
(approximately 15 types of activities would be listed here)			

that all those who execute these plans be in on the planning and be aware of what is going on. This adheres to the management principle that those people who are affected by a decision should be the ones to actually make the decision. That is the key to enthusiasm and support by the people. With Key Result Areas and objectives in mind, the various strategies are agreed upon. They are listed immediately under the objectives. Next, all the "actions" that must take place must be listed. Also note in each example exhibit the areas to write in who is in charge, date started, and date completed. Consider as well what resources each action will require.

These documents become not only a guide to action but provide a timeline for starting and completing plans. The person or persons responsible and the expected date of completion must be agreed upon. Every person involved gets a copy of the plan with his or her areas of responsibility marked. Now one person can coordinate a multitude of projects and programs, because there is a clear record of what is to be

Exhibit 7.7. Action Plan for Financing/Development for a K-12 Academy

---

KEY RESULT AREA: Improve the financial condition of the Academy through increased giving and improved enrollment (new and retention).

OBJECTIVE: Increase giving to both Capital and Operational Budget from $200,000 to $300,000 per year.

STRATEGIES:

    A. Develop the "case" or "story" of the academy and identify 12 projects ranging from $1,000 to $100,000 to present to foundations

    B. Develop proposals for grants

    C. Develop an alumni survey and telephone campaign

ACTION PLAN	PERSON RESPONSIBLE	START DATE	DATE COMPLETED
Send letter to all private foundations in the state			
Call on executive directors of the five "connected" foundations			
Write an appeal letter to alumni			
Personally visit every person who has given in excess of $2,500 in the past			
Arrange speaking engagements at each of area "service clubs"			

---

done. As each action or task is completed, the person responsible sends in a completion report. The coordinator (or planning team leader) knows what is going on all the time with this approach.

Periodic updates of the action plan are carried out so that everyone sees the progress. After people become accustomed to using the action plan format, they discipline themselves. They do not want others to see that they are falling behind. This is a great time saving and coordination format. Appendix C presents a sample strategic plan to illustrate the development of strategies to accomplish a mission.

SUMMARY

A well-thought-out plan suggested by everyone succeeds. How many times do you see educational institutions trying to do everything at once? The word "strategic" in the title of this book implies thinking, planning, and seeking order and priorities. All this can happen if an action plan coordinates and supports the overall plan.

NOTES

1. For additional discussion of this topic see Kotler, Phillip, and Andreasen, Alan R. *Strategic Marketing for Nonprofit Organizations*, Prentice-Hall, Inc. Englewood Cliffs, New Jersey, 1987, pp. 188-190.
2. Ibid. pp. 182-184.

STRATEGY DEVELOPMENT WORKSHEET

This worksheet is provided to help you develop a strategy for your educational institution.

Answer these questions first:

1. What are the distinctive competencies of your institution? What do you do well that makes you different from other higher education institutions?

    _____

    _____

    _____

2. What market segment or segments should you select to match your institution's skills and resources and constituents' needs in those segments?

    _____

    _____

    _____

3. Do you have the skills/resources to pursue several segments or should you concentrate on one segment? Are the financial sponsorship and funding opportunities of that segment large enough to sustain your institution and allow for growth?

    _____

    _____

    _____

Now, develop your positioning statement:

1. Distinctive Competencies

    _____

    _____

    _____

2. Client Segments Sought

_____

_____

_____

3. Services Offered

_____

_____

_____

4. Promotion Orientation

_____

_____

_____

5. Financial Support Levels

_____

_____

_____

6. Growth Orientation

_____

_____

_____

Next, develop your overall strategy (Growth, Stability, Retrenchment) for each major program:

Major Program_____

<u>Growth (add or expand spectrum of programs)</u>

    Growth: alternative strategy 1

Pros	Cons
1.	1.
2.	2.
3.	3.

    Growth: alternative strategy 2

Pros	Cons
1.	1.
2.	2.
3.	3.

<u>Stability (keep same programs while improving on effectiveness and efficiency)</u>

    Stability: alternative strategy 1

Pros	Cons
1.	1.
2.	2.
3.	3.

    Stability: alternative strategy 2

Pros	Cons
1.	1.
2.	2.
3.	3.

Retrenchment (major reduction or elimination in existing programs)

Retrenchment: alternative strategy 1

Pros	Cons
1.	1.
2.	2.
3.	3.

Retrenchment: alternative strategy 2

Pros	Cons
1.	1.
2.	2.
3.	3.

Recommended overall strategy for each program

Program:_____

Justification: explain why this is the best alternative.

Pros	Cons
1.	1.
2.	2.
3.	3.

Finally, establish operational strategies for objectives in each Key Result Area in each major program that supports your overall strategy for that program.

An action plan for each Key Result Area should be developed. The action plan places Key Result Areas, objectives, strategies, and action plans into perspective with each other and helps you develop the interrelationships among plans at each institutional level. It helps goals come to life with appropriate action.

ACTION PLAN

OBJECTIVE:_____

_____

STRATEGIES:

    A. _____

       _____

    B. _____

       _____

    C. _____

       _____

    D. _____

       _____

    E. _____

       _____

ACTION PLAN:_____

_____

_____

_____

Person
Responsible:_____

Resources
Required:_____

Date
Started:_____

Date
Completed:_____

Chapter 8

Evaluation and Control Procedures

What gets measured gets done.

—Mason Haire

. . . precisely because the bottom line is not a measure of accomplishment, everything becomes a moral absolute.

—Peter Drucker

Institutions of higher education . . . "neither minimize nor maximize costs; instead, they operate within a range of accepted norms for production relationships, such as student-faculty ratios or lab space per student for instruction."

—Paul Brinkman

The evaluation and control stage of the strategic planning process can be compared to setting out on a journey with a road map. The process includes recognizing the desire to take a trip (Key Result Area), identifying your destination (objective), determining the best route to your destination (strategy), and then departing for your trip (implementation of your strategy including an action plan). During the journey, you look for highway signs (feedback) to tell you if you are on the way to your objective. Signs and early warning signals along the way quickly reveal if you have made a wrong turn, and you can alter your course to get back on the right road. When you reach your destination, a new route (strategy) is needed to get you to new destinations which are part of your Key Result Area and objective.

Imagine what would happen if there were no road signs during your trip to let you know if you were on the right road. It might be too late to continue the trip by the time you realized you were traveling in the wrong direction. Yet, many private higher education institutions are involved in a similar situation, failing to analyze key signs and milestones along the way toward determining if objectives are being accomplished.

Failure to establish procedures to appraise and control the strategic planning process can lead to less than optimal performance. The poor financial condition of many private higher education institutions is prime evidence that average performance is not acceptable as an operating norm. Thus, many institutions fail to understand or appreciate the importance of establishing procedures to appraise and evaluate the implementation stage of the planning process. This chapter reviews the need for evaluation and control, explains what is to be evaluated, and offers some control procedures. Evaluation and control should be a natural follow-through in developing a plan as discussed in Chapter 2. No planning process should be considered complete until evaluation measures are identified and the procedures for recording and transmitting control information to administrators of the planning process are established.

INTEGRATION OF PLANNING AND CONTROL

Planning and evaluation/control should be integral processes. In fact, planning is defined as a process that includes establishing a system for feedback of results–mid-course results as well as end results. This feedback reflects the institution's performance in reaching its objectives through implementation of the strategic plan. The relationship between planning and control is depicted in Exhibit 8.1.

The strategic planning process results in a strategic plan. This strategic plan is implemented (activities are performed in the manner described in the plan) and results are produced. These results include such things as educational programs delivered; services rendered; gift and grant income; and accompanying student (and other stakeholders') outcomes, attitudes, preferences, and behaviors. Information on these results and other Key Result Areas is

Exhibit 8.1. The Planning and Control Process

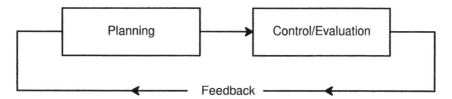

given to faculty and administrators, who compare the actual results with planned objectives to evaluate performance. This evaluation identifies the areas where performance is either acceptable or not acceptable according to predetermined standards. In the Key Result Areas where performance is not acceptable, decisions must be made to adjust curriculum, programs, activities, facilities or other resources, people, or finances. The actual decision making controls the plan by altering it to accomplish the mission, the Key Result Areas, stated objectives, strategies, and the action plan. Timely and accurate information flows are the key to a good control system.

The last stage of the strategic planning process, then, is to appraise the institution and each of its entities (departments, schools, colleges as applicable) to determine if all objectives have been met satisfactorily:

- Have the measurable objectives and goals been accomplished?
- How close did actual performance attain the mark?
- Did the attainment of the objectives and goals support the overall mission of the institution?
- Has the external environment or internal culture changed enough to change the mission, Key Result Areas, or objectives?
- Have additional weaknesses been revealed that will influence changing the mission of the institution?
- Have additional strengths been added or has the institutional position improved sufficiently to influence the changing of your mission?
- Has the institution provided its members with institutional rewards, both extrinsic and intrinsic?
- Is there a feedback system to help members satisfy their high-level needs?

Timing of Information Flows

The strategic plan is supported by an action plan. We plan for the long run, but must operate in the short run with an eye to the long run. If each of our action plans is controlled properly and in a timely manner, the strategic plans are more likely to be controlled. The college or university administrator cannot afford to wait for the time period of a plan to pass before control information is available. The information must be available within a time frame which is long enough to allow results to accrue, but short enough to allow actions to adjust and to align results with objectives.

Most private institutions in higher education can adequately control operations with monthly or quarterly reports. Cumulative monthly or quarterly reports become annual reports, which in turn become the feedback needed to control operations according to the strategic plan. Deciding what information is provided to which faculty and administrators in what time periods is the essence of a control system.

PERFORMANCE EVALUATION AND CONTROL

Performance should be evaluated in many areas to provide a complete analysis of what the results are and what caused them. Four key control areas are enrollment management, academic affairs (faculty, programs, and curriculum), financial affairs (donations and business office), and stakeholders' attitudes–especially students and alumni. Objectives should have been established in all of these areas for the strategic plan.

Enrollment Management Control

Enrollment management control measures are provided by the marketing and admissions departments of the institution through an analysis of quantitative and qualitative data on inquiries, applications, acceptances, and enrollment. Detailed analysis might include enrollments by:

- Academic program, academic level, and part-time/full-time status

• Gender, age, income, geographical distribution, and other demographic and psychographic characteristics

Enrollment can be evaluated on a program-by-program basis by developing a performance report as shown in Exhibit 8.2. When such a format is used, the enrollment objectives stated in the plan are analyzed by breaking down the annual objectives by semester and then by program. These data become the standard against which actual enrollment results are compared. Number and percentage variations are calculated, because in some instances a small percentage can mean a large number in variation.

A performance index can be calculated by dividing actual attendance by the attendance objective. Index numbers near 1.00 indicate that expected and actual performance are about equal–a sign that performance is under control. Numbers larger than 1.00 indicate above-expected performance, and numbers below 1.00 reveal below-expected performance. Index numbers are especially useful when a large number of programs are involved, because indexes enable administrators to identify those programs which need immediate attention.

Academic Affairs Evaluation

Several key factors need to be collected and analyzed in the Key Result Area of academic affairs: competent and effective faculty, access to adequate library and learning resources, appropriate computer resources, and instructional materials and equipment. As an example, Exhibit 8.3 shows a faculty performance evaluation report for faculty in a certain department or school (using a format similar to the enrollment performance report in Exhibit 8.2).

Exhibit 8.2. Enrollment Performance Report, Fall Semester (by program)

Education Program	Enrollment Objective	Actual Enrollment	Variation	Percent Variation	Performance Index
A	500	430	− 70	− 14.0	.86
B	95	102	+ 7	+ 7.4	1.07
C	120	92	− 28	− 23.0	.77
D	200	240	+ 40	+ 20.0	1.20

Exhibit 8.3. Faculty Summary Teaching Performance Report for the Academic Year Ending (date)

Faculty Member	Faculty Development Performance Plan Objectives	Actual Performance Evaluations	Percent Variation	Performance Index
A	100	104	+ 4.0	1.04
B	100	101	+ 1.0	1.01
C	100	97	− 3.0	.97
D	100	112	+ 2.0	1.12
E	100	94	− 6.0	.94

Departmental Faculty Performance Index (Average) 1.016

Some systems of faculty performance planning and evaluation allow for a mutually agreed upon faculty development plan which has measurable elements. The quantified objectives are then converted to a composite totaling, say, 100 points. The exhibit uses a composite of 100 for each faculty member but that need not be the case. Any amount can be set. The only requirement is that a faculty member can exceed or fall short of the composite objective. While most faculty evaluation experiences are challenging at the least, this probable Key Result Area is at the center of the mission of the educational institution. Effective evaluation and control requires finding a workable way of completing this part of the strategic planning process. All parties to the faculty evaluation process should have input to the design and implementation of the faculty teaching evaluation report.

Financial Cost Controls

Various stakeholders are interested in the financial soundness of the institution–both at present and in the near future. Several tools are available for establishing cost control procedures and standards, including budgets, expense ratios, and activity costs analysis. Budgets are a common tool used by many educational institutions for both planning and control. The budget is often established by using historical percentages of various expenses as a percent of revenues. Thus, once the total level of expected donations is established, expense items can be budgeted as a percent of total revenue.

If zero-based budgeting is used, where each period's budget is developed from scratch without benefit of last period's budget, the objectives to be accomplished must be specified and the expenditures necessary to accomplish these objectives estimated. The estimates are the budgeted expenses for the time period.

Donations or contributions are monitored by tracing gifts on a periodic basis, usually at least monthly. Many private higher education institutions have annual drives by selected type of donor such as alumni, major donors, corporate donors, and the like. A prerequisite to controlling contributions is an annual projection of operating revenues and expenses. This projection, broken down on a quarterly or monthly basis, becomes the standard from which deviations are analyzed. For example, a private college or university with a projected budget of $24,000,000 for the next fiscal year might have the following expectations based on historical trends and patterns:

- Tuition, fees, and miscellaneous income account for 80 percent or $20 million in operating revenue.
- Contributions to the operating fund, some 20 percent or $5 million in revenue, tend to be realized fairly evenly throughout the year with slightly higher amounts in November and December.
- Budgeted expenses tend to be spread evenly during the 12-month period, or $2 million per month.

If there were large variations related to certain times of the year, even the variations can be analyzed to determine the proportion of the budgeted amount received per month. If, historically, 20 percent of the $5 million budget was donated during December, then 20 percent of next year's budget becomes the expected level of donations to be used as the standard.

The same type of analysis used to control enrollment (shown in Exhibit 8.2) can be used to analyze data on revenues. This type of analysis should be performed on a timely basis to enable expansion or cutbacks of variable expenses and/or programs when revenue levels go above or below the expected amounts for the period.

Once the budget is established, expense variance analysis by line item or expenditure category is used to monitor costs. A typical procedure is to prepare monthly or quarterly budget reports showing the amount budgeted for the time period and the dollar and percentage variation from the budgeted amount, if any exists. Expenditure patterns which vary from the budgeted amounts are then analyzed to determine why the variations occurred.

Another control tool involves the use of financial ratios and activity percentages. The ratios and percentages presented in Exhibit 8.4 can be used to make comparisons against established objectives in each category, prior year's ratio performance, and typical ratios and percentage indicators for the industry (Robinson, 1990, pp. 2-3).

Larger educational institutions find revenue/expense centers a useful tool in control. For example, a university generates revenues through tuition and fees by college, school, and department. Revenues and expenditures for on-campus and distance education programs can be separated. Computer services can be viewed as a unit which serves such "customers" as various academic and administrative departments. Tracking these revenues and expenses in a cost center would help control this service by letting the administrator know if it is operating at break-even or if it is generating excess revenues which could lead to expanding the service, lowering the price of interdepartmental services, or using the surplus for other services.

Stakeholder or Constituent Feedback

Another key area of performance evaluation is various stakeholders or constituents, and involves analysis of awareness, knowledge, attitudes, and behaviors of students, alumni, or financial supporters. Every institution should want its constituents to become aware of programs, services, or personnel; possess certain knowledge; and exhibit certain attitudes and behaviors. If these are specified, as they should be, in the objective statements, these objectives become the standards against which current constituent data can be compared.

Data on constituents must be collected on a regular basis. There are many ways to collect data, but annual surveys are commonly used. Constituent data are especially valuable if collected over a long period of time, because awareness levels, satisfaction, attitudes, and behavior can be analyzed to reveal trends and areas for further investigation.

Exhibit 8.4. Financial and Activity Ratios and Percentages

Revenue Ratios and Indicators
- Tuition and Fees as a Percentage of Total Revenue
  Note: Total revenue = tuition and fee income + private gifts, grants, and contracts + endowment income + auxiliary income + government grants and contracts
- Private Gifts, Grants, and Contracts as a Percentage of Total Revenue
- Endowment Income as a Percentage of Total Revenue
- Sales and Services of Auxiliaries as a Percentage of Total Revenue
- Revenue per FTE Student: Total Revenue/Total FTE students

Expenditure Ratios and Indicators
- Instructional Expenditures as a Percentage of Total Current Fund Expenditures: instructional expenditures/total current fund expenditures
  Note: Total current fund expenditures = expenditures for instruction + academic support + student services + institutional support + plant operations and maintenance + auxiliaries
- Academic Support Expenditures as a Percentage of Total Current Fund Expenditures
- Institutional Grant Aid as a Percentage of Tuition and Fee Income
- Percentage of Regular Faculty Salaries Offset to Research

Balance Sheet Ratios and Indicators
- Current Fund Balance This Year as a Percentage of Current Fund Balance Last Year
- Long-Term Debt as a Percentage of Total Liabilities
- Assets as a Percentage of Total Liabilities
- Endowment as a Percent of Total Assets
- Endowment per FTE Student
- Total Return on Endowment
- End-of-Year Market Value of Total Endowment as a Percentage of Beginning-of-Year Value

Fundraising and Development Percentages
- Annual Fund Dollars as a Percentage of Total Dollars Raised
- Gifts and Grants from Foundations as a Percentage of Total Dollars Raised
- Gifts and Grants from Corporations as a Percentage of Total Dollars Raised
- Percentage of Alumni Who Have Given at Any Time During the Past Five Years

Enrollment Percentages
- Percentage of Inquiries Who Applied
- Percentage of Applicants Who Accepted
- Percentage of Accepted Students Who Matriculate
- Percentage of Students Who Are Part-Time

Exhibit 8.4 (continued)

Faculty and Staff Indicators
- Percentage of FTE Faculty Who Are Part-Time
- Percentage of FTE Faculty Who Are Tenured
- Ratio of FTE Students to FTE Faculty

Liquidity Ratios
- Cash Ratio (cash and cash equivalents/current liabilities)
- Current Ratio (current assets/current liabilities)
- Current Asset Ratio (current assets/total assets

Operating Ratios
- Net Operating Ratio (excess of income over expenses/total revenue)
- Fund Balance Reserve Ratio (total fund balance/total expenses)
- Cash Reserve Ratio (total cash/total expenses)
- Program Expense Ratio (total program expenses/total expenses)
- Support Services Ratio (total support services expenses/total expenses)

Analysis across the key control areas often provides comprehensive measures of effectiveness and are summary indicators of operational performance in relation to the strategic plan. Relating enrollment, faculty, and financial data will provide comprehensive key "road signs" on the way to institutional objectives. Thus, student/faculty ratios, tuition revenue generated by each faculty member, and tuition revenue (less unfunded financial aid) per FTE (full time equivalent) student are examples of comprehensive control measures.

ESTABLISHING PROCEDURES

It should be pointed out that none of the performance evaluation data described are going to be available unless they are requested and funds are made available to finance them. Thus, data collecting and reporting procedures must be set up by the administrators who are going to use the control data in decision making.

The procedures will usually change over time as new types of analysis or reporting times are found to be better than others. The most important requirement is that the data meet the needs of administrators in a timely and cost-effective manner as they determine to take corrective actions to control activities. With the expanded availability and use of computers by educational institutions, much of the work can be computerized.

PERFORMANCE EVALUATION GUIDELINES

Several summary guidelines should be kept in mind when establishing an effective system for performance evaluation:

1. Performance evaluation must be primarily self-evaluation.
2. Performance evaluation is for healthy, performing, growing individuals.
3. Evaluation should use both objective and subjective measures.
4. "No evaluation" is not an option.
5. When an evaluation process is perceived as legitimate, fair, and working, people will tend to use it responsibly. When it is not, people will still do something, but they might not feel the burden of responsibility to do more than is absolutely required.
6. Performance evaluation is a formal process (that is, it should be documented).

The evaluation and control system in general should:

1. be linked to strategy;
2. be simple and economical to use;
3. measure both activities and results;
4. flag the exceptions;
5. focus on key success factors, not trivia;
6. be timely;
7. be flexible as strategy changes with environmental demands; and
8. be reality-based where written reports are augmented by face-to-face follow-up (the idea behind MBWA–management by walking around).

It is in the appraisal and control stage that educational institutions really begin to see the benefits of the strategic planning concepts outlined in this book. When people at all levels know the progress being made toward fulfilling the overall plan, it creates a sense of pride, accomplishment, and excitement. Strategic planning will not work well without a review of performance.

SUMMARY

No planning process should be considered complete until evaluation and control procedures have been established and implemented. Without such information, it is impossible to manage an educational institution's performance with any sense of clarity about what is actually happening in the institution.

Performance evaluation is vital for control decisions. Information tells an administrator what has happened, and serves as the basis for any actions needed to control the activities of the institution toward predetermined objectives.

CONCLUSION

The thoughts we have offered throughout this book, we believe, will help make your private higher education institution more effective. In the end, an institution thinking about implementing a strategic planning program should consider the following points:

1. The decision to implement this management philosophy should not be made in haste.
2. To the extent possible, it must receive the support of the faculty, president, and board of trustees.
3. It is strongly recommended that some type of training session take place in a retreat environment.
4. An outside resource person (consultant) could be very useful in getting the program started and then to keep it on schedule and a high priority.
5. When applicable, a person from the institution who can take over as the in-house expert (or at least liaison) should be assigned to work with the consultant.
6. Each institution must find the best way for its people to review its mission, set Key Result Areas, and determine objectives and an action plan.
7. Each institution should come up with its own best method for handling feedback and reviews.
8. Be prepared to expose your management team to new ideas and new ways of approaching managerial problems.

9. Ways should be found to involve all employees in some decision making.
10. Personnel performance reviews must be conducted at regular, scheduled intervals.
11. Be prepared to spend time and hard work keeping the program viable, especially in the first six months.
12. Every institution and each of its decentralized entities can adopt a system of setting objectives within the mission statement to its situation.
13. Objectives must be negotiated rather than imposed unilaterally by the administration or Board.
14. Periodic reviews of strategic plan progress are a must and the review must include the president.
15. Both extrinsic and intrinsic rewards must be obtainable by the individual and the group in which he or she works.
16. Use methods that require a minimum of paperwork for setting, reviewing, and updating Key Result Areas and objectives.
17. Don't let a staff department (support area) dominate the strategic plan of the institution.
18. Involve all stakeholders in the strategic planning process.

May your institution's future be one that is enhanced by a well-developed and effectively implemented strategic plan.

EVALUATION AND CONTROL WORKSHEET

This worksheet will aid you in developing tools to measure progress toward your institution's Key Result Area objectives.

Answer the following questions:

1. What kinds of information do you need to evaluate a program's or service's success?

   _____

   _____

   _____

2. Who should receive and review this information?

   _____

   _____

   _____

3. What time periods do you want to use to analyze the data? Weekly? Monthly?

   _____

   _____

   _____

4. What record-keeping system do you need to devise to make sure the information you want is recorded for the time periods you specified in question 3?

   _____

   _____

   _____

Now set up your control procedures:

1. Specify the areas to be controlled:

   A._____

   B._____

   C._____

   D._____

2. Specify the format of the data for each area. (Is it to be numbers by month by program? Do you want number and percentage variations?)

   A._____

   B._____

   C._____

   D._____

3. Specify how the data are to be collected, who is to collect and analyze the data, and who is to receive the results of the analysis:

   A. How will the data be collected?

   _____

   _____

   _____

   B. Who has responsibility to collect and analyze the data?

   _____

   _____

   _____

C. Who is to receive which type of analysis?

Office   Type of Analysis

_____   _____

_____   _____

_____   _____

_____   _____

4. How will the evaluation take place once the analysis of data has been completed?

_____

_____

_____

Appendix A

Case Study: Strategic Planning at Thorndyke College

President J. Henry Singleton returned to his office on December 15, having just left a long three-day planning retreat with the Thorndyke Board of Trustees. As he leaned back in his desk chair, he reflected on the proceedings and concluded that he would have to deliver a "good-news, bad-news" report to the College faculty and staff in three weeks when all would be returning from Christmas holidays. Henry was pleased with the Board Chairman Richardson's moving speech at the conclusion of the retreat. He reread the Board Resolution which gave him authority to move on new program initiatives in the areas of distance education and degree completion. A smile broke across his face when he recalled that Board Chairman Richardson became enthusiastic in his proposals and led discussion to fund these new initiatives. Within a few minutes, Board members pledged $200,000.

However, problems also emerged from the meeting. The Board had, of course, shared the president's concern about admissions and the progress of both the operating fund and the capital campaigns. But no one had proposed programs or even ideas for dealing with problems in these critical areas. Approval of the new initiatives and the immediate substantial financial response was very encouraging—they represented dreams of innovative programs he would liked to have implemented three years ago when he had come to the College. However, they would not be a substitute for the application and enrollment problems experienced with on-campus traditional programs or the funds for much needed facilities and equipment. Of course, he did not need to be reminded of the need to supplement faculty salaries and benefits. His thoughts turned to the Board's charge of a fully completed strategic plan presented at the Fall Board meeting. This plan had to include a fundraising program to bring long-run stability to the College. He was pleased that he had foreseen the strategic planning assignment and was well "down the road" toward completion of the data and information collection stage. He had a little over nine months to get the plan into presentable form for the October 4-5 Fall Board meetings.

HISTORY

In 1911 a group of ministers began discussing the need to establish a college to be located in Thorndyke, a city at that time of 25,000 mostly middle-class people. The motive of the ministers was clear–provide an alternative to the state university where questionable moral values were taught and modeled. Most people in Thorndyke shared the desire to send their young people to an educational institution with a mission, faculty, and curriculum that was distinctively different from that being offered at the state university located 75 miles away. The ministers were able to gain the attention of several prominent citizens of the community and shared their idea with them. Together they began to plan how they might have a college in Thorndyke. By 1913 there was a fund of $75,000 set aside and the promise of the availability of a suitable facility from the City. Formal incorporation of the College came about and a group of seven local men were asked to be on the Board of Trustees. A president was found who shared the values of the founders and he began the process of organizing the College, finding faculty, and recruiting students. While war was beginning in Europe, 21 students enrolled for the first time in the fall of 1914. Thorndyke College was a reality.

The study of the classics and moral issues dominated the curriculum in the early years. During the 1920s several other majors were added and the number of students grew to 73 by 1925. Several had graduated and gone on to the state university for graduate studies. The town was very proud of the College.

Finding funds was difficult during the 1930s, but the College hung on with a small cadre of students and some dedicated professors. Recovery started to come with a greater number of female students during World War II. After the war there were some veterans and the number of young people expanded as well. The College reached an enrollment of 268 by the fall of 1948. The College now had seven majors and a number of new professors began to bring change to Thorndyke College. The third president came in 1949 and his vision of the College was to make admissions selective and to emphasize the liberal arts. The original focus of the classics and morality were seldom discussed anymore. The faculty and staff saw themselves as being much like the other liberal arts colleges in the State. By 1959 the enrollment had passed 600.

During the years following, Thorndyke copied other liberal arts colleges as much as possible and became a composite of what other small liberal arts colleges were like throughout the United States. An exchange program was developed, new majors were added, and new professors came to teach the growing population.

By 1979 the College began to see that the future was not going to be as good as the past 30 years. The fourth president of the College suggested that the College needed to plan due to changes taking place. For example, he had read about new demographic patterns that would hurt enrollment at the College. He predicted that unless the College was able to design and implement a plan, they would not be able to attract students in the quantity and quality that had kept Thorndyke financially viable. The discussion about planning, however, turned out to be an opening of the school year speech that was largely forgotten as the year progressed.

During the 1980s the College had arrived at an organizational pattern of five divisions:

- Humanities
- Physical and biological science
- Social science
- Health, physical education, and recreation
- Professional studies (teacher education and business)

Departments were informal within these divisions. There was little change in the College's vision from the end of the war to date. Faculty goals related to better pay, more frequent sabbaticals, and more library holdings. Enrollment had dropped to the low 400 range. At the same time, the financial condition had deteriorated and the 1980s were a time of wondering whether enough resources could be found to keep the College in operation.

By 1990 enrollment had increased slightly to 450 and remained at that level for the next five years. Most people had a theory about the cause of the enrollment drop and most had a solution to suggest. There was little consensus in either the conclusion about causes or the remedy.

THE PAST THREE YEARS

President J. Henry Singleton had come to the College three years ago, from a previous position as executive vice president of a medium-size southwestern university. His enthusiasm about the challenge of taking a small college and leading a turnaround caught the appreciation of some key college stakeholders. Now, looking back, he saw the last three years as a long, hard effort which was just recently yielding fruit (see Appendix A-1: Exhibits 1 through 5). For example, the gradually declining trend in enrollment had subsided with three fairly good years of on-campus growth. The financial hemorrhaging had been stopped with significant improvement in this area due in part to aggressive tuition increases (with enrollment growth) and aided by a freeze on faculty salaries for two consecutive years.

SHORT-TERM ACTIONS

When he arrived on campus, Henry Singleton initiated what the business world calls "reengineering the organization." He streamlined the administrative support staff, and had committees review every policy and procedure in both the faculty and the staff employee handbook (with many subjects referred to committee for study and recommendations for change). Henry made several personnel changes in key positions resulting in a "flat" organization structure. He wanted the administration to take the lead in being effective.

Then he took a hard look at the faculty and staff. He froze faculty salaries for two years with no new tenured appointments. He adopted a divisional structure with division heads and eliminated several department chair positions. This enabled him to justify the elimination of some expensive, low enrollment "majors." He worked with Board Chairman Harold Richardson in expanding and broadening the base of the Board of Trustees. Also, he engineered a committee structure of the Board which mirrored the administrative and academic structures operating at the College level. These initiatives, adopted over a period of 18 months, began to change the culture of the institution. President Singleton hoped that these changes would be perceived by external stakeholders (especially donors and prospective students) as positive steps to revitalization of the College—and worthy of a successful marketing and public relations campaign resulting in increased fundraising and enrollment.

RESPONSES TO CHANGE

Changes affected some parts of the College more deeply than others. Traditional students, of which there was a recent enrollment decrease, did not seem to promise the future enrollment growth needed. It was the nontraditional student market which generally affirmed the direction the College should strongly consider. Most of the new students were older, worked part-time or full-time in the community, and were looking for career enhancing education. However, complaints from this group of students began to surface. Their concerns focused on the inconvenient daytime, residential student class-time schedules.

Faculty, many disgruntled from the two-year salary freeze and the elimination of "majors," found the changes they were experiencing disturbing as well. Under the previous administrations, the full-time faculty had regarded itself as a family. By regional standards they had always been paid well below the average, but they enjoyed the teaching conditions of small classes and highly-motivated students. For these members of the faculty, the new administration's "reengineering" program brought austerity without the favorable teaching conditions. In addition, faculty could see that they would be asked to teach evening classes (and possibly weekends) in the near future.

Thorndyke alumni had varied responses to the changes recently instituted–mostly following age/time of graduation. Recent graduates responded enthusiastically. One 1989 graduate wrote:

> It is timely to make changes responding to the needs of today's students, many of us have to work in order to make it through; it looks like you are trying to be "user friendly" to this growing segment of the population. I hope you realize that nontraditional education is here to stay and will become the significant part of future growth.

The opposite attitude prevailed among graduates of the College from the 1950s through the 1970s. Many older alumni and parents of recent graduates found the changes unsettling. They felt that the value of Thorndyke degrees were being "watered-down" with more emphasis on getting jobs rather than understanding the classics in a small class setting with faculty time available for mentoring. One perceptive alumna criticized the elimination of the science majors in Physics and Chemistry. She said, "It's like we are reverting back to the 1950s 'Sputnik Era' when the Soviet Union surpassed the United States in the physical sciences."

The Board of Trustees generally supported the new administration. They knew the difficult financial situation when President Singleton took the reins. One trustee commented that there were a lot of people around who were suspicious of anyone who was an outsider to the Thorndyke community (J. Henry Singleton was the first president who had not grown up in or around the local area). "Henry Singleton," he said, "has an excellent track record of sensing the needs of both students and donors and using those needs to drive changes in the way we structure and deliver education."

Singleton appreciated the general support he felt from the Board, but he was concerned that most were passive in recommending solutions, particularly in dealing with the difficult problems of enrollment and funding.

STRATEGIC PLANNING

In the early months of the new calendar year, President Singleton, anticipating Board of Trustee action in the near future, began to prepare the College for strategic planning. With the implementation of his short-term "reengineering" strategy, his thoughts turned to the bigger picture and the long run. At a meeting of his Cabinet he formed a planning committee which he called the Strategic Planning Task Force (SPTF). The task force was a broad-based group composed of students, faculty, administration, and staff; there were even two Board of Trustee members as well as a couple who were faithful donors to the annual fund of the College. As they gathered for their first meeting, one of the members made the point, "We have spent all of our energy and resources trying to 'put out fires' and taking actions to turn the college around. Why should we get involved with planning when we don't have a clear idea of what our mission is or where the financial resources are coming from to implement plans?" There was agreement that this was a good question. Henry was grateful for the comments; these were his exact sentiments and the extra benefit was that they were expressed by a member of the faculty rather than by him.

So in March, President Singleton asked Academic Vice President George Fuller to chair the Strategic Planning Task Force. Immediately the SPTF became known as the Fuller Committee (a reflection of the high respect the Thorndyke community had for Dr. Fuller). They were to report back to President Singleton by the second week in September. The specific charge to the Fuller committee was fivefold:

1. "To review the College's vision statement and mission statements taking appropriate action in proposing changes as deemed necessary."
2. "To identify any key issues discerned throughout the process of interviewing stakeholders and collecting information."
3. "To collect and synthesize facts, figures, interviews, responses, and suggestions of a wide scope of individuals, groups, and data sources within Thorndyke College, in the local community, and encompassing the larger geographic market area in which the college competes for most of its students. Then develop a document which clearly states the environment and competitive position of Thorndyke College."

4. "To determine feasibility of any new programs that might help future prospects for enrollment growth."
5. "To develop a Strategic Planning Calendar."

At a general meeting of the faculty and staff of the College that afternoon, President Singleton introduced the "Fuller Committee" and commented that "you will be hearing much about strategic planning in the near future. One of the key steps in the strategic planning process includes scanning the external environment and internal organization for facts, analyzing and assessing the data, and relating conclusions to the mission, goals, strategies, and action plans of the College. You will likely be called upon to provide strategic planning-related information; please cooperate with these fine servants who have taken this job over and above their regular duties and responsibilities."

STRATEGIC PLANNING TASK FORCE

By the middle of October, much of the interview work and other data collection of the task force had been completed. It was handed over to the College planner who added appropriate information her office collected on an on-going basis; results of all data and information were then summarized in a report format and reviewed by the Fuller Committee. Vice President Fuller presented President Singleton with an executive summary which showed the Strategic Planning Task Force findings:

- Five Strategic Planning Issues Identified (see Appendix A-2)
- Vision, Values, and Proposed Revised Mission Statements (see Appendix A-3)
- Environmental Scan and Analysis (see Appendix A-4)
- Some Proposed New Initiatives to Improve Future Enrollment Growth (see Appendix A-5)
- Proposed Strategic Planning Calendar (see Appendix A-6)

Henry was delighted with the information; he would include it as part of the upcoming Board of Trustees planning retreat.

BOARD OF TRUSTEES PLANNING RETREAT:
DECEMBER 13 to 15, 1995

Desiring to involve the Board of Trustees in planning, Singleton invited them to a three-day retreat in mid-December to discuss the future direction of Thorndyke College. In his letter of invitation, the President stated two specific objectives to be accomplished at the planning retreat. First, he wanted the Trustees to fully comprehend the need to design and implement a viable, consistent, long-term financial strategy. The short-term "turn-around" successes in enrollment and financial conditions were just that—short-term. Thorndyke's financial position was still seriously weak as revealed in the attached Administrative Report–Key Result Areas (see Appendix A-1, Exhibits 1 through 5). Second, he desired that the Trustees, recognizing the implications of the financial situation, would consent to explore with him a range of alternatives the College might consider. In fact, he hoped that some specific direction might come forth during the retreat.

Opening Remarks

President Singleton opened the formal part of the retreat with a frank assessment of the financial condition and student recruitment outlook of the College (see Appendix A-1, Exhibits 1 through 5). "In summary," he said, "the last three years the College has experienced what can clearly be called a financial turnaround. However, it was done so at the expense of faculty salaries and significant increases in enrollment which cannot be sustained in the future without some new program initiatives."

Henry went on to point out that the condition of both the buildings and grounds was such that deferred maintenance could not be continued without serious consequences. Then there was the great need to catch up in the area of educational technology, especially computers, to support the students, the library, the staff, and the faculty.

Capital and Endowment Funds Request

He finished his opening statement with a bold request for funds:

> To pursue the kinds of initiatives to move this institution to the next level of quality and financial stability (and move it

away from being an indistinct little liberal arts college with a questionable future), we would need 'seed capital' to start up new initiatives and restore some deferred maintenance and equipment expenditures.

In addition, he proposed the need for $25 million of endowment. The income would meet increased ongoing operating costs. Singleton concluded:

> It is time for the Trustees and the administration of Thorndyke College to give more than passing consideration to a wide range of College needs and some new initiatives. During the next three days, we are not engaged in a mere exercise in dreaming and creative fundraising, but a question of competitive positioning and perhaps survival.

Strategic Planning Task Force Report

Before breaking up into smaller groups and discussing the merits of these proposed initiatives and/or any initiative yet to be proposed by the Board, Singleton had arranged with Board Chairman Harold Richardson to allow Vice President Fuller to present his Strategic Planning Task Force Report. Vice President Fuller distributed five documents and gave a brief report on each document:

1. Strategic Planning ISSUES (See Appendix A-2)

The Fuller Committee Report discussed five key issues that have been uncovered during the past eight months:

a. Incongruence between mission and new program initiatives.
b. Low job placement rate of College graduates.
c. Target market of traditional students–should we expand?
d. Nontraditional programs and delivery systems–many colleges are adapting to changing student needs.
e. Narrow funding base.

Most of these issues relate to changes taking place in the student market and their educational needs.

2. Proposed Thorndyke College MISSION/VISION
(See Appendix A-3)

As the Board of Trustees know, the following statement was presented to and accepted by the Board upon the inauguration of Dr. Singleton as the seventh president of Thorndyke College. The SPTF finds no reason to change this vision statement:

> The vision of Thorndyke College is to become one of the 100 best liberal arts colleges in the nation through excellent programs for deserving and motivated students taught by faculty with the finest credentials who are focused upon the quality of teaching.

However, the College will need to develop short-term and long-term financial structure to encourage and fund these activities. The management and Board of the College must maintain the vision before all constituent groups while providing efficient and effective management of the resources toward accomplishment of the vision.

3. Environmental Facts and Analysis (See Appendix A-4)

At President Singleton's direction, the committee has collected and analyzed data in ten areas of our environment–the external and internal include:

1. Academic Affairs
2. Recruiting/Enrollment
3. Institutional Advancement
4. Financial Affairs
5. External Environment and Competitive Institutions
6. Student and Alumni Affairs
7. Athletics
8. Physical Plant
9. Auxiliary Activities
10. Technology and Nontraditional Education

A summary of each data category is shown in Appendix A-4.

4. Proposed New Program Initiatives (See Appendix A-5)

The Strategic Planning Task Force identified 15 key people with whom ideas about new programs were discussed in depth; this group included the President, the Academic Vice President, key department chairs, and several educators outside the College. Each of the following four initiatives were considered as marketable and fit within the vision and proposed mission of the College. For each of the proposed initiatives, we conducted a market and economic feasibility study including projected initial start-up costs and annual operating revenue and expense estimates:

- Degree Completion Program in Human Resource Development
- Offer existing programs at off-campus locations in the community
- Branch campus in a large city on the other side of the state
- Distance Education Program

The detailed version of these subcommittee reports will be available for Board Member review in the office of the Academic Vice President. Estimated start-up costs and annual operating revenues and expenses are shown in Appendix A-5. The faculty are aware of these initiatives; any faculty member who might be affected has had an opportunity for input. Upon Board approval of any one or more of these new initiatives, the administration will notify the appropriate accrediting organizations.

5. Finally, Dr. Fuller Shared His Committee's Comments on the Fifth Document—A Proposed Strategic Planning Calendar to Be Used Each Year (See Appendix A-6).

Chairman Richardson thanked Dr. Fuller for the informative presentation on the work of the Strategic Planning Task Force. The Chairman then asked President Singleton if he wished to comment. Henry Singleton responded in the affirmative and said:

First, I wish to publicly commend Vice President Fuller and his committee for the excellent work accomplished to date. The committee performed this work in nine months that would normally take twice that long. We now have much valuable information, most of which has never been collected before, on which to pull together a strategic plan which we propose to be presented at the Fall Board of Trustees meeting in early October.

"Are there any questions about Dr. Fuller's report or President Singleton's remarks?" asked Chairman Richardson. One member asked if it was reasonable to assume that these new initiatives would generate excess revenues over expenses once start-up costs had been incurred. President Singleton assured the Board that the detailed feasibility studies available in Dr. Fuller's office had been reviewed by several knowledgeable people. The projections of initial start-up costs, along with operating revenues and expenses, have been acknowledged as reasonable and "doable."

Seeking Strategic Direction from the Board

Chairman Richardson indicated he was moving to the next agenda item. Again, he turned to President Singleton to lead the discussion. President Singleton explained:

> What is needed now is direction from this Board in the form of a reaffirmed vision statement, an approved mission statement, and some kind of action on the five issues that have surfaced. I am hoping that you will take favorable action on what has been presented to you. With your permission, I will summarize the agenda for the two days remaining in this Board retreat.

Chairman Richardson followed with a resounding, "By all means." President Singleton continued:

> Over the past year I have been seeking counsel on the topic of "strategic direction" for the College, that is, how we should position Thorndyke College to bring more permanent stability in the areas of finances and enrollment. The alternatives that seem to keep coming to the surface are:
>
> 1. Begin immediately to pursue the nontraditional market niches, especially evening adult learners who are demanding a variety of educational programs—evening programs, degree completion programs, and distance education programs.
> 2. Enter into a collaborative program with the local state university to share resources and costs in selective high cost majors.

3. Expand our degree offerings to the graduate level with a branch location in one of three promising cities on the other side of the state.
4. Seriously consider a possible merger with another institution.

I have concluded that alternatives numbered 2 and 4 above are only last resort measures. With regard to alternatives numbered 1 and 3, we have engaged in extensive research and feasibility study.

President Singleton then continued:

Dr. Fuller has presented you with information which in large part will become the essential elements of our strategic plan. We do not have the luxury of waiting until the next Fall Board meeting to review the completed plan as a prerequisite to making some important strategic direction decisions.

I now refer you to a key information item—Appendix A-4: Environmental Scan and Analysis. The source of this information comes out of our College planning department with some primary research input from the Fuller Committee reports. Appendix A-4 summarizes the College's opportunities and threats in the external environment and its strengths and weaknesses inside the organization. A review of these data has led me to an alarming conclusion: *The College does not have a focused strategic direction, especially in light of the proposed mission statement. In addition, we do not have a strong competitive position when viewed in the context of where private higher education is moving—nontraditional and consumer oriented.*

After some heated discussion among Board members, a majority of the Board agreed with Singleton, and the president continued:

My response to these conditions and circumstances as your President is to offer three strategic direction-related resolutions for your discussion and hopeful approval:

Resolution No. 1

Be it resolved that the vision statement be reaffirmed and the proposed mission statement as presented in Appendix A-3 of the SPTF Report be adopted as official foundational documents of the institution.

The College cannot proceed with strategic planning without either changing the mission statement or changing our operations to conform to the old mission statement.

Resolution No. 2

Be it resolved that the five issues listed and evaluated as Appendix A-2 in the SPTF Report be adopted as official guidelines in setting goals and objectives, in crafting strategy, and making and implementing action plans as part of the overall Strategic Plan of Thorndyke College.

Resolution No. 3

Be it resolved that the administration is authorized to act on each of the four proposed initiatives stated in Appendix A-5 of the SPTF as, if, and when the start-up monies are on deposit in the bank.

President Singleton then concluded, "With these resolutions, I rest my administration's case. I need your counsel and support on whatever action items/resolutions the Board of Trustees passes during this retreat."

Day Two of the Retreat

When the meeting was opened for Board participation, the Trustees first discussed the administrative reports dealing with the "Big Two"–Fundraising and Student Recruitment.

When details were pursued about admissions applications for the new academic year, a significant decline was revealed in comparison to the three previous years. One thought from a Trustee, put in the form of a suggestion, was that the admissions staff needed to be expanded since it was obvious that the admissions office was not contacting enough prospects. Other Trustees were not convinced that this was the solution; perhaps the problem ran deeper than that.

Chairman Richardson redirected discussion to the Fuller Report (SPTF) summarizing the five issues (Appendix A-2) and the proposed mission/vision statement (Appendix A-3). Discussion heated up as Trustees expressed many opinions both as to the veracity of the issues as well as their causes. The newer members of the Board that had been elected since Henry Singleton became President seemed to rally around the need to bring significant change. Trustees who had been on board for several years tended to become somewhat defensive of past policies and programs leading to the current situation. Chairman Richardson encouraged the spirited discussion while seeking ways to build consensus through "win-win" strategies. At the end of the second day of the retreat, Richardson attempted to summarize the day's deliberations:

1. A clear consensus exists that the College does not have clarity of vision/mission among the various stakeholders, including the Board of Trustees.
2. The nature, composition, and characteristics of our customer base (students) seems to be changing; President Singleton is proposing the College make appropriate programmatic changes to better fit these changing needs. Underlying this point is a major unresolved issue that the Board must face: Do we change and, if so, in what direction?
3. Recruiting information is alarming; our weak financial position is even more precarious in light of the status of applications for enrollment next fall.

The final day of the planning retreat was begun on a somber note. The agenda called for action on President Singleton's proposed resolutions as well as the capital and endowment requests. The Trustees debated each of President Singleton's requests. Many of the Trustees were not sure whether the College should venture into nontraditional education; it seemed to them that we were getting away from our original purpose of preparing full-time, in-residence undergraduates for further study and/or leadership roles in society.

Concern was raised about the job placement situation; no one seemed to have any ideas to solve the problem. A number of the members pointed out that major changes in programs would change the nature of the faculty and student body. One Trustee asked the question: "Is it possible these changes would negatively impact the alumni and have an adverse effect on fundraising?" This group believed that Thorndyke College should continue to position itself in the future much as it had in the past–a small, liberal arts, residential, regional college.

At this point the Board went into executive session and excused President Singleton and Vice President Fuller. By the close of the session, Chairman Richardson's deft people skills had brought a general consensus among Board members. Resolutions were passed which directed President Singleton:

1. With regard to the five issues presented in the Fuller Report:

   - Issue # 1: Do not continue.
   - Issue #2: Conduct a study to determine the facts connected with alumni perceptions; include your findings in a report to the Board in October and take findings into consideration in the strategic plan.
   - Issue #3: The College must "broaden the tent pegs," that is, expand the vision to be more inclusive.
   - Issue #4: Initiate a pilot nontraditional educational program, such as a degree completion program or branch locations, just as long as it fits within the strategic plan. A separate plan of action is to be presented at the October Board meeting.
   - Issue #5: Long-term financial stability is of utmost importance to the Board. The funding base must be broadened; our fundraising strategies must be updated.

2. With regard to affirming the vision statement and adopting a new mission statement, Chairman Richardson reminded the Board that President Singleton's vision statement, which has not changed, was fully affirmed by this body some three years ago. The proposed mission statement is more closely aligned with the vision statement than our historic mission statement.

The environmental scan data seem to support the proposed mission statement. Again heated debate took place, but in the end, the proposed mission statement was passed with a surprising large majority. (See Appendix A-3.)

3. Include in the strategic plan a detailed action plan to bring long-run financial stability to Thorndyke College. You may include any of your stated alternatives/new initiatives except merger with another institution. If you and your colleagues propose a collaborative effort, demonstrated commonality of values and shared vision are musts.

Before concluding the three-day planning retreat, Chairman Richardson made a rare personal position statement about the College. He said,

I feel compelled to share with you my personal, professional opinion about our deliberations. As you know I have served this institution as Trustee for some 18 years, the last five of which I have been privileged to be the Chairman. Knowing the responsibility of this position, I have tried never to abuse the trust you have placed in me. However, I have been greatly encouraged over the past three years during what can be called a significant turnaround. By and large, I believe President Singleton has provided strong leadership and made some tough decisions which have not made everyone pleased. My background as a businessman allows the same conclusion as Henry's; we are not financially sound. I will add that we will not make it unless we respond to the marketplace with bold changes requiring much better counsel and more fundraising help than we, as a Board, have given the College in the past. I can't help but become excited about the nontraditional initiatives that Henry is proposing and we have affirmed with supporting resolutions. I regret that I have not shared my personal convictions formally to the Trustees before. Perhaps I am out of order, but I would like to poll this Board about challenging and authorizing President Singleton to design and implement one of those nontraditional programs this fall. I'm willing to back up my convictions that we must not dally by making a financial pledge today!

Order was almost lost at the conclusion of Richardson's personal appeal. Quite a few Trustees voiced the affirming "Hear, hear!" phrase often heard in the English parliament. Within five minutes, over $200,000 was pledged by a dozen Trustees. Then someone offered a resolution to authorize President Singleton to launch the program as soon as the pledges had become reality in the form of a balance in a special bank account.

The resolution was amended, with no objection, to add an accountability sentence requiring a detailed action plan to be approved by the Trustee's Executive Committee prior to committing funds beyond those required for essential planning.

PRESIDENT SINGLETON'S RESPONSE

Driving to the campus the next day, Singleton called his executive assistant and asked her to clear his calendar for the afternoon. He had some heavy thinking to do—without interruption. Upon arriving at his office, he began to write down several key questions that needed answers:

1. How should he incorporate the newly Board-authorized "Degree Completion Program" into the yet to be completed Thorndyke College Strategic Plan?
2. What should be done about planning for student recruiting and admissions?
3. Which has higher priority—the operating fund or the capital campaign?
4. What new personnel with what skills and competencies will be needed to implement new programs and initiatives authorized by the Board of Trustees?

Appendix A-1

Administrative Report:
Key Result Areas (Thorndyke College)

Exhibit 1. FTE Enrollment*

Year	Total Enrl	Full-Time	Part-Time	Female	Male	Average at Comparable Institutions
1960	645	615	30	345	300	n.a.
1965	685	660	25	365	320	n.a.
1970	590	560	30	335	255	n.a.
1975	550	500	50	320	180	n.a.
1980	410	335	75	250	160	n.a.
1985	430	345	95	265	165	n.a.
1990	450	340	110	270	180	n.a.
1992	450	320	130	260	190	763
1993	475	300	175	270	205	820
1994	510	300	210	290	220	860
1995	550	320	230	310	240	900

*Full-time equivalent (FTE) = 12 semester hours/headcount

Exhibit 2. Tuition and Fees

Year	Thorndyke College	Average at Comparable Institutions
1990	$5,700	$5,514
1991	5,700	5,965
1992	6,500	6,338
1993	6,900	6,971
1994	7,400	7,555
1995	7,900	8,000 (est.)

Exhibit 3. Summary Revenue and Expenditure Statements, Current Fund ($000)

	Actual 91-92	Actual 92-93	Actual 93-94	Actual 94-95	Actual 95-96
REVENUES:					
Tuition and Fees	2,565	2,925	3,277	3,774	4,345
Less Fin. Aid (unfunded)	600	200	100	50	25
Net Tuition and Fees	1,965	2,725	3,177	3,724	4,320
Scholarships (funded)	200	200	180	180	180
Gift Income	2,174	1,901	2,200	1,800	1,800
Other Income	40	43	45	45	45
Total Revenues	4,379	4,869	5,602	5,749	6,345
EXPENDITURES:					
Instruction	1,782	1,634	1,634	1,793	1,947
Academic Support	450	500	500	500	500
Student Services	490	610	600	450	450
Institutional Support	1,620	1,900	1,950	2,000	2,200
Plant Operation	575	400	730	850	900
Scholarships	200	200	180	180	180
Total Educ/Genl	5,117	5,244	5,444	5,773	6,177
Bookstore/Housing	40	50	50	50	50
Other	20	0	0	0	0
Total Expenditures	5,177	5,294	5,594	5,823	6,227
EXCESS REV OVER EXP	(798)	(425)	8	(74)	118

Exhibit 4. Faculty Salaries

Year	Thorndyke College	Average at Comparable Institutions
1990	$25,800	$33,600
1991	$27,000	n.a.
1992	$27,000	n.a.
1993	$27,000	n.a.
1994	$28,600	n.a.
1995	$29,500	$40,000 (est.)

Exhibit 5. Endowment and Gift Income

Year	End-of-Year Endowment	Annual Gift Income
1960	$1,750,000	$1,000,000
1965	1,850,000	1,300,000
1970	3,500,000	850,000
1975	3,500,000	1,850,000
1980	3,800,000	2,200,000
1985	3,850,000	1,300,000
1990	3,925,000	1,250,000
1995	3,950,000	1,400,000

Appendix A-2

Strategic Planning Issues
by Strategic Planning Task Force
(Thorndyke College)

1. Historically, the College tended to develop programs to fit donor's needs and the current president's agenda. The committee's evaluation is that this practice is not driven by the mission of the College and seems to be "shallow fundraising strategies." *ISSUE: Should the College continue this practice in the future?*

2. Alumni are finding it increasingly more difficult to find employment leading to leadership positions in most sectors of the society. Consequently, there has been a noticeable change in enrollment patterns from the traditional liberal arts, to the professional areas including business, helping professions, and information management. The committee's evaluation is that there is a mismatched curriculum in relation to perceived student needs. *ISSUE: Should the College realign its majors and programs to meet these perceived needs?*

3. Over the years, we have "prided ourselves" on being a residential, undergraduate college seeking to attract above-average-income households. Today there is an unstable quantity and uneven quality of student enrollment. *ISSUE: If we expand our target market to a broader income range and pursue adult education programs, will we lose this strength?*

4. Adult learning in general and demand for degree completion programs in particular seems to be a concern of people over the age of 30. The committee's evaluation is that there is a mismatch

between current curriculum content and delivery and perceived student needs. The faculty seems unsure about expanding into nontraditional educational programs and delivery systems. *ISSUE: Should we consider responding to this market niche? To do so means we will increase the evening academic activity, offer classes off campus and perhaps open branch locations in other cities.*

5. Primary funding from major donors and most of the "regular donors and casual contributors in the past has been from loyal, conservative, wealthy families located within 150 miles of the campus." Past presidents and development vice presidents have maintained this focused funding strategy. The committee's evaluation is that our funding base is too narrow to meet the present and future financial needs of the College. *ISSUE: Should we broaden the funding base for both major donors and "regular donors?"*

Interviews from among the various stakeholders indicated faculty are about equally divided favoring and not favoring a proactive move on the five issues. In addition, there seems to be a general sense of fuzziness with regard to the strategic direction of the College; until that issue is resolved, one seasoned faculty was quoted as saying, "How can we get enthused about a change in curriculum, student demand, delivery systems, and so forth when there has been no clarity of direction for many years?"

Appendix A-3

Report on Vision/Mission by Strategic Planning Task Force (Thorndyke College)

The vision and mission statements of Thorndyke College were found to be known by less than half of the various stakeholders interviewed. It was recalled by many that President Singleton has shared the vision of the College in numerous speeches and public gatherings, but people were uncertain what the vision statement contained. In fact most indicated they had never seen it in writing. When the mission statement was read to them, most people indicated that the current status and future outlook of the College from their perspectives did not adequately agree with the College's mission statement. In July, President Singleton called together leaders from various stakeholders/constituencies of the institution for a planning retreat to review the vision statement and revisit the mission statement.

In the case of the vision, a substantial majority of the retreat participants were enthusiastically behind the vision statement. Chairman Fuller voiced the majority opinion: "Keep the Vision Statement as it is but communicate it more frequently both verbally and in writing."

THE VISION FOR THORNDYKE COLLEGE

The vision for Thorndyke College is to become one of the 100 best liberal arts colleges in the nation through excellent programs for deserving and motivated students taught by faculty with the finest credentials and who are focused upon the quality of teaching. The College will need to develop short-term and long-term financial structures to encourage and fund these activities. The management of the College must maintain the vision before all constituent groups while providing efficient and effective management of the resources toward accomplishment of the vision.

The committee also collected and listed a set of institutional values that various constituents of the College held strongly and which have clearly become a part of the culture of the College community.

KEY INSTITUTIONAL VALUES

Underlying the College's vision/mission are the following values and beliefs which serve as the foundation for the organization's culture and provide a basis for alignment in assessing the mission:

- Quality in teaching, research, and service
- Quality in programs and learning environment
- Access to all qualified students who want to learn
- Diversity and multiculturalism
- Curriculum–relevant, mission-focused, and integrated
- Effectiveness and efficiency
- High-touch and high-tech
- Community outreach
- Global scope
- Judeo-Christian values of personal integrity and work ethic

The Committee spent most the retreat working on revising the Mission Statement with the intent that it more adequately reflects "who we are." The results of that retreat follow.

PROPOSED REVISED THORNDYKE MISSION

THE MISSION: Thorndyke College is committed to providing a high-quality educational experience grounded in the tradition of liberal arts education and specialized programs that provides "cutting edge" skills and competencies for selected professions. The College provides liberal arts education leading to undergraduate degrees, diplomas, and certifications and is receptive to meeting the learning needs of students as life-long learners in the United States and in selected foreign countries. The College is committed to growth and development of the whole person–spirit, mind, and body–to be accomplished in both the traditional on-campus environment and through nontraditional education using a balance of "high-touch" and "high-tech" methodologies and delivery systems. Graduates will thereby be equipped to pursue further study, life-long learning, leadership, and service to society.

While the Committee recognizes the newly proposed mission statement is longer than normal, participants felt the need to reflect the input of the entire group. The Thorndyke mission statement reflects commitment to educating with a purpose to serve and lead in a global context undergoing rapid change. This commitment of educating for leadership and service in a rapidly changing world is matched with just as strong a commitment to hold to traditional values on which the College was established over 80 years ago.

Appendix A-4

Environmental Scan and Analysis by Strategic Planning Task Force (Thorndyke College)

This document provides subcommittee reports on the current status of the College in ten areas of the external and internal environment. The document was prepared by College staff for the Strategic Planning Committee.

1. Academic Affairs

   - Have 60 FTE faculty (50 full-time and about 20 part-time).
   - Morale of faculty is mixed; some still upset about salary freezes in 1992 and 1993.
   - Organized into six divisions, with 25 areas of specialization (no majors, which has several faculty upset).
   - Use of computers and technology in the classroom is not a reality; computer literacy is low except among the younger and/or newer faculty and staff.

2. Recruiting/Enrollment

   a. Student Recruiting

      - The short-term strategy for student recruitment has been very successful; however, it cannot be sustained for very long into the future.
      - Enrollment growth rates have exceeded the average of comparable institutions in the region over the past three years.

- Older, nontraditional students make up the large majority of the new growth in student enrollment.
- Unless a change to more user-friendly programs and student support services is instituted, the nontraditional student source of growth may falter, especially in light of potential competition of more aggressive institutions.

b. Enrollment

- Over 20 percent growth in the last three years, which is a significant turnaround. (See Appendix A-1, Exhibit 1.)
- Most of the new growth has been with nontraditional students (average age over 30, most working full-time, all need greater flexibility in class scheduling).

3. Institutional Advancement

- New Vice President of Advancement (Fundraising and Public Relations).
- Gift income has remained stable over the past three years, which is a turnaround from the gradual decline of the past two decades. (See Appendix A-1, Exhibit 5.)
- Overall cost of fundraising and student recruitment has increased, but cost per student recruited and enrolled has decreased.

4. Financial Affairs

- Significant improvement in financial condition over the past three years (see Appendix A-1, Exhibit 3) due primarily to significant enrollment increases of nontraditional students and significant reduction in pay raises.
- Faculty salaries are in the lowest 25 percentile relative to comparable institutions in our region; fringe benefits for faculty and staff are well below comparable institutions which will make it difficult to hire faculty for any new initiatives the Board authorizes to strengthen the College's overall competitive position.

- Endowment has not grown in any appreciable amount for the past decade.
- Cash reserves are low and the financial vice president finds it necessary to borrow in the summer months to meet payroll.

5. External Environment and Competitive Institutions

Most competitive institutions are pursuing new initiatives in the areas of programs, admissions, and/or fundraising. Those who are not doing so seem to be stagnating. Within a 100-mile radius, there are two private colleges which are proactive in adding some kind of a nontraditional learning component to their programming. Rumor has it that one institution has retained a consultant to develop a degree completion program in the area of business and human resource management. Various media covering the city of Thorndyke offer advertisements to local College-eligible students to attend the state university and some eight private institutions, including out-of-state institutions offering degrees by correspondence.

6. Student and Alumni Affairs

a. Currently enrolled students

- Most students like the changes that have taken place in the past three years.
- Increasing number of complaints about availability of computer courses and equipment.

b. Alumni

- Alumni seem to have mixed feelings about the changes that have taken place during the past three years.
- Of those graduating during the past five years, 97 percent are employed, but only 60 percent are employed in a job for which they were trained in school; increasing number of complaints on this topic.

A sample of employers returned a questionnaire concerning their satisfaction with the job performances of Thorndyke graduates who began employment with them within the past five years. A majority of the respondents graded our alumni above average to excellent for those who had gone on and earned a graduate degree from another college or university, but only 30 percent of the respondents gave a rating of above average or excellent to those graduates without further academic training.

7. Athletics

Since the College is not engaged in intercollegiate athletics, no report is offered on this topic.

8. Physical Plant and Grounds

- The College is without a current master facilities plan.
- There is evidence of significant deferred maintenance among many of the older buildings on campus.

9. Auxiliary Activities

Dorms, cafeteria, bookstore and other auxiliary services seem to be adequate according to a student questionnaire on these topics. Financially, the College barely breaks even on auxiliary enterprises.

10. Technology and Nontraditional Education

- Except for a few notable cases, faculty are computer illiterate.
- While all appropriate staff have computers, most are a generation or two behind state-of-the-art equipment.
- Technology in the classroom does not exist at Thorndyke College.

Most new student enrollments are classified as nontraditional. Currently there is little competition in the city of

Thorndyke, although there are rumors that two or three regional institutions are considering opening branches to serve the older student population.

Appendix A-5

New Program Initiatives (Proposed) (Thorndyke College)

To respond to the changing student markets and needs of the community and beyond, some new programs should be considered. As a result of surveying various stakeholders and conducting feasibility studies, the SPTF proposes the following:

1. Begin a "Degree Completion Program in Business Management and Organizational Management." There are several reputable consulting firms and educational institutions which provide whatever knowledge and skills that the College lacks to design, implement, and operate such a program. Estimated start-up costs are $200,000. This program can be launched almost any time of the year. From the beginning, this program will result in a net excess of revenue over expenses after the first year.

2. Offer our undergraduate business administration program at one or more corporate locations within the Thorndyke market area. Start-up costs estimated at $50,000; it may take two years to get to break-even situation with revenues and expenses.

3. Open a limited branch campus in a large city on the other side of the state. This initiative is more difficult to estimate start-up and operating revenues and expenses since competition is stronger in the bigger cities. Estimated start-up costs are $200,000.

4. Design and implement a "Distance Education Program" for students seeking master's level teaching credentials in any state of the United States. Potential excess revenues are very high. Estimated start-up costs are $350,000.

Appendix A-6

Strategic Planning Calendar (Proposed) (Thorndyke College)

(Fiscal Year begins on July 1)

Month	Step	Strategic Planning Activity/Event
Sept.	1	Strategic Planning Task Force (SPTF) identifies potential goals based on Board of Trustees' statement of mission and guiding principles.
Oct.	2	SPTF receives environmental analysis data collected by the College planner. Reviews external opportunities and threats, internal strengths and weaknesses.
Nov.-Dec.	3	SPTF recommends College goals, objectives, and College-wide strategies, taking into consideration mission, feasibility, trends, and organizational strengths; sets tuition rates for next academic year.
Jan.-Feb.	4	Step 3 recommendations communicated to various College stakeholders for feedback; adjustments recognized and each planning unit (academic, academic support, and administrative support units) directed to set goals, objectives, strategies, and action plans consistent with approved College-wide targets.
Mar.	5	Each planning unit completes strategic plan along with a plan to monitor and evaluate actual progress toward achieving goals and objectives.
April	6	Sets detailed budget for each planning unit.
May	7	Board of Trustees approves strategic plan and budget.
May-June	8	Identifies and procures human and financial resources necessary to implement the strategic plan.
July-June	9	Implements strategic plan, monitors and evaluates results, and updates action plans accordingly.

Appendix B

Strategic Plan Outline

Using the information developed with the strategic planning worksheets, your strategic plan can be compiled. Plan descriptions can take many forms. (Note sample plan in Appendix C.) One useful approach is captured in the following outline.

I. Executive Summary

- Highlights of each of the following plan sections (1-2 pages)

II. Vision Statement/Mission Statement

III. Overview of Overall Strategies and Strategic Objectives

1. Description of major challenges and problems facing the institution.
2. Description of major assumptions on which the strategic plan is based.
3. Summary of Key Result Areas as they relate to mission and challenges noted describe how Key Result Areas:
   a. capitalize on distinctive competence and key strengths
   b. manage around or improve on major weaknesses
   c. overcome major external threats
   d. tap key opportunities
   e. fulfill the mission statement and are consistent with the vision statement

IV. Strategic Plan Implementation: Operational Objectives and Strategies by Program or Service

1. Program 1 (as many Key Result Areas as desired)
   a. Key Result Area 1
      (1) major objective 1
         • strategy 1 description to achieve major objective 1
         • strategy 2 description to achieve major objective 1
         • evaluation and control standards and time frames
      (2) major objective 2
         • strategy 1 description to achieve major objective 2
         • strategy 2 description to achieve major objective 2
         • evaluation and control standards and time frames
   b. Key Result Area 2
      (1) major objective 1
         • strategy 1 description to achieve major objective 1
         • strategy 2 description to achieve major objective 1
         • evaluation and control standards and time frames
      (2) major objective 2
         • strategy 1 description to achieve major objective 2
         • strategy 2 description to achieve major objective 2
         • evaluation and control standards and time frames

2. Program 2 (as many Key Result Areas as desired)
   a. Key Result Area 1
      (1) major objective 1
         • strategy 1 description to achieve major objective 1
         • strategy 2 description to achieve major objective 1
         • evaluation and control standards and time frames
      (2) major objective 2
         • strategy 1 description to achieve major objective 2
         • strategy 2 description to achieve major objective 2
         • evaluation and control standards and time frames
   b. Key Result Area 2
      (1) major objective 1
         • strategy 1 description to achieve major objective 1
         • strategy 2 description to achieve major objective 1
         • evaluation and control standards and time frames
      (2) major objective 2
         • strategy 1 description to achieve major objective 2
         • strategy 2 description to achieve major objective 2
         • evaluation and control standards and time frames

V. Summary and Conclusion

- Highlights of plan's key points showing how they successfully deal with major issues and problems of the institution and fulfill on-going mission.

Appendix C

Sample Strategic Plan
for Department of Business
(Thorndyke College)

This is a strategic plan for the Department of Business, Thorn-dyke College. This plan will not include or analyze the past events (external, internal, and assumptions) which have led to the current situation of the unit. This is well-documented in other reports prepared by Thorndyke business faculty and the College's office of institutional research. Instead this plan is future-oriented and will cover the following elements:

1. Purpose/Mission
2. External/Internal Analysis and Assumptions
   (see College Strategic Plan)
3. Key Result Areas
4. Goals/Objectives
5. Strategies
   Positioning
   Leadership/Faculty/Curriculum
   Business Leaders
6. Operational Plans
   Manpower Plan
   Implementation Timeline
7. Evaluation and Control (Financial Analysis)

This proposal concentrates on the overall grand strategy for the Department. Supporting strategies for recruitment of faculty, students, Business Advisory Board, and endowments would also need to be developed and implemented to carry out the overall strategy.

Purpose/Mission

The mission of the Department of Business is to contribute to the overall Statement of Purpose of the College–"to provide a high quality educational experience grounded in the tradition of liberal arts education and specialized programs that provide 'cutting edge' skills and competencies for selected professions." The challenge to the programs of the Thorndyke College Department of Business is to pursue educational excellence while developing proper attitudes toward people, spiritual matters and integrity of character, and physical wholeness.

Specifically, our programs are: committed to extending the values and traditions of Thorndyke College through service to people in the marketplace wherever leadership, organization, and other business skills are needed worldwide; and dedicated to providing trained, academically qualified leadership for profit and nonprofit organizations which include large and small business, churches, service organizations, the academic community, government, health care, and other areas which can benefit from business concepts and managerial skills. The graduates must be making worthy contributions as accomplished professionals in both their professional and personal lives. We have an obligation to a wide community which includes our students, fellow faculty, the general public, our academic peers, service organizations, the government sector, health care, churches, and small businesses.

We aspire to develop graduates who are able to lead and manage with a balanced "high-touch and high-tech society" and whose personal lives and philosophies reflect strong moral values. Additionally, we desire to develop the conviction that they have an obligation to help right what is wrong in the world about them.

Finally, we want to be an integral part of the local and regional, consulting, and economic development. We want to be a source of quality students who seek advancement in their companies. We want to be thought of as "*The* School of Business" for this region.

Objectives (Nonquantifiable)

1. Maintain and enhance the objectives outlined in the current strategic plan of Thorndyke College.

2. Produce quality graduates, both undergraduate and eventually graduate, who are prepared to work in today's economic environment.
3. Develop a placement program so local and national recruiting efforts will be made to hire Thorndyke College graduates.
4. Develop a sense of community image in the region (i.e., the city of Thorndyke and the region are proud of Thorndyke College; community and regional leaders turn to the Thorndyke Department of Business for help in solving community and marketplace needs; regional businesses respect the talent in the Thorndyke College Department of Business from both faculty and students).
5. Become *the* business school in the region area, then in the state and beyond (i.e., awards, published articles, books, press releases).

Objectives (Quantifiable)

1. Provide a steady increase of 3 percent per year in credit hours generated.
2. Increase the number of undergraduate business students to 50 full-time and 50 part-time by Fall 1998.
3. Complete one community research project each year.
4. Make a positive contribution to overall College overhead costs by 1997.
5. Sponsor at least three continuing education/executive development seminars on campus each year.
6. Receive AACSB (American Assembly of Collegiate Schools of Business) provisional accreditation by 2000; full accreditation by 2003.

Positioning Strategy

The Department of Business should be positioned relative to other business schools as a quality program in a values-and-servant-attitude environment which emphasizes developing analytical skills, leadership skills, and communication skills within a framework of high ethical standards. The business program should differentiate itself through innovative courses and experiences provided for students. The emphasis should be on building a quality program rather than a quantity program based on large numbers of poorly qualified students. The success of the program would enable an expansion of the size of the program, but only if additional faculty were hired.

The business program offers potential for interfacing with the business community, local and state government offices, and other like-minded service organizations and institutions. Such interfaces, if effective, can create opportunities for employment, research/consulting, service, and endowment funds.

The interfaces are possible through both undergraduate and potential graduate programs with the difference being the level at which such interfaces occur, i.e., MBA faculty/students can create opportunities to interface with senior executives. Therefore, both a strong graduate and undergraduate program are essential to maximize the impact of the Department of Business on these various constituents.

Leadership/Faculty/Curriculum Strategy

The foundation of any educational system is the quality of the faculty and the appropriateness of the curriculum. Students are both customers and products of the educational system. The higher the quality of the students entering the program, the higher the quality of the end product.

Overall, the current faculty in the Department of Business are high-quality people in terms of commitment to excellence, character, teaching strength, and moral character. However, what is missing is creative leadership in the Chair's position and terminally qualified faculty teaching upper level, undergraduate, and graduate courses. (A terminally qualified business faculty is someone with a PhD or DBA in business or someone with a doctorate in another area who can be judged terminally qualified based on teaching and/or business experience.)

The Department of Business needs to hire a qualified Chair who can provide creative leadership and build the team effort needed to accomplish the Department's objectives. This has to be the number one priority in terms of the success of the business program and should be implemented as soon as possible, preferably before Fall 1997.

In addition, at least one more qualified faculty member should be hired by Fall 1997 to teach both undergraduate and proposed graduate courses. If the right person were hired, this would improve the quality of the program and increase the proportion of the senior/ graduate level courses taught by qualified faculty. This person should be committed to quality teaching and to the research/writing which is expected of qualified faculty. As the program grows, additional faculty will be needed who are terminally qualified and can provide leadership in teaching, research, and service for their disciplines.

Proposed Changes to the Undergraduate Curriculum

Establish immediately a working committee to research the needs of our undergraduates from the perspective of employers of our graduates; also identify core courses and electives best suited for our graduates who go on to graduate school. Committee needs to be mindful of identifying "niches" in the market so as to position the program to attract the best quality students.

The current curriculum for the graduate program needs to be designed to make it competitive and also reflect current changes and deficiencies in other business programs. These weaknesses include (1) lack of training in how to provide leadership in vision, communication, implementation, and self-management; (2) developing an ethical framework for decision making; and (3) being mentored by an executive role model in the art of working with and through people. The following curriculum would offer such needed changes.

Proposed MBA Curriculum

Core courses (27 hours) required for all students:

1. Strategic Management
2. Managerial Accounting
3. Managerial Finance
4. Marketing Management

    5. Business Research Methods
    6. Statistics/Computer Applications
    7. Organizational Behavior
    8. Executive Development (leadership skills development and ethical decision making)
    9. Internship (mentoring by a qualified business executive)

Electives (6 hours) to be selected from such courses as:

    1. Entrepreneurship
    2. Bank Management
    3. Investments
    4. Services Marketing

The first seven required courses reflect the common body of knowledge of the business curriculum. The last two, Executive Development and Internship, are designed to overcome weaknesses in most MBA programs.

The program would require a total of 33 credit hours beyond the undergraduate business degree and no written thesis. The research and writing skills would be developed through the other courses.

This proposed new MBA curriculum will be a significant part of the Department of Business's total positioning strategy and has the promise to attract students, faculty, and support for the program. The mentors (executives) would be recruited through the local and regional business community. An innovative idea that needs to be researched is to institute a mentoring program through the Internet; the Hewlett Packard Corporation has pioneered this concept at the elementary and secondary school level.

Business Leaders' Strategy

To be effective, a business program needs constant interaction and feedback from business leaders who ultimately pass judgment on business programs–both undergraduate and graduate–by supporting or not supporting the programs. Their support comes from hiring graduates, providing internships, research/consulting opportunities for faculty, and through gifts and endowment support. The Thorndyke College Department of Business needs to develop a

Business Advisory Board made up of local and regional business executives who can serve as strong role models and who will make a commitment to helping develop a quality business program.

This board would meet on a regular basis and provide input on curriculum, course design, and internships/mentorships. They could also serve as guest lecturers in classes and become a "sounding board" for ideas on programs and fundraising. Their input into the program would help establish their "ownership" of the program, and this would motivate them to help ensure its success. They would also be a source of mentors for the proposed MBA program.

Organizational Structure

The current organizational structure is inadequate to serve the needs of an innovative and growing program. Therefore, the organizational structure shown in Exhibit C.1 is proposed to help implement the strategies previously outlined.

Under this design, the Chair of the Department of Business would report to the Dean of Academic Affairs. The Chair would provide overall leadership for the Department; recruit faculty; and interact with the College administration, the Business Advisory Board, other business and community leaders, and Department of Business administrators, faculty, and students.

The Associate Chair would manage the internal affairs of the Department and also manage the Department's student recruitment activities and continuing education program. The Associate Chair would also teach graduate and undergraduate courses and manage department activities such as budgeting, scheduling, and advising and take an active role in recruiting faculty. The Free Enterprise Chairholder would teach one course each semester and be responsible for helping the Chair in acquiring student internships, working with the Business Advisory Board, grant writing, helping to prepare grant proposals to fund action-oriented research, and help manage business/community leader relationships.

Manpower Plan

If a new Chair who was terminally qualified in either accounting or marketing were hired by Fall 1997 and taught one course a

Exhibit C.1. Organizational Structure: Department of Business,
Thorndyke College (Proposed)

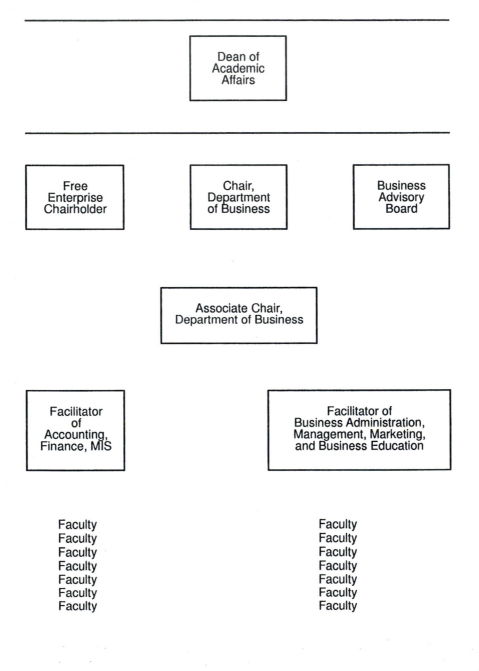

semester, the addition of one new terminally qualified faculty member by Fall 1997 would cover the courses in the proposed MBA program, assuming no current faculty resigned.

Depending on the disciplines of the new Chair and new faculty member, 90 percent to 100 percent of the MBA courses would be taught by qualified faculty. There would also be an increase in the proportion of upper level undergraduate courses taught by terminally qualified faculty. The addition of a faculty member and streamlining of the curriculum would provide availability of doctorally qualified faculty for undergraduate courses.

The teaching loads for the administrators/faculty would be as follows:

Position	Teaching Loads
1 Chair	3 hours per semester
1 Associate Chair	6 hours per semester
1 Free Enterprise Chairholder	3 hours per semester
2 Facilitators of Discipline Areas	6 hours per semester
2 Full-Time Graduate/ Undergraduate Faculty	9 hours per semester
10 Full-Time Undergraduate Faculty	12-15 hours per semester

Four terminally qualified faculty members who are committed to teaching and research would need to be hired—one person per year beginning the Fall of 1998—for the next four years in order to make appropriate progress toward the long-term goal of AACSB accreditation. The Department needs more terminally qualified faculty teaching upper level courses and needs to maintain AACSB standards for FTE faculty per student hours taught.

One basic misconception perpetuated by the current budget centers is the separation of graduate/undergraduate faculty/budgets. If other private or state educational institutions kept graduate faculty, students, and expenses separate, their programs would also show a loss for graduate hours generated. No department of business separates the two cost centers. Faculty members are hired to teach in the Department of Business, and if they are terminally qualified they are appointed to the graduate faculty. The AACSB requires that a significant proportion of the upper level undergraduate courses be taught by terminally qualified faculty. At the present time only two of the 13 full-time faculty have terminal degrees in business. Any terminal degree outside business has to be justified as to why that person's degree should be considered terminal in terms of teaching experience, business experience, and research/writing in his or her area of teaching.

It seems unwise to separate the two units by administration, cost centers, budgets, or any other factor which causes the units to appear to stand alone. While the undergraduate program appears to be making a positive contribution after covering its expenses, it does so only because of the lack of terminally qualified faculty who command much higher salaries than the current undergraduate faculty. So the undergraduate program's positive contribution financially is achieved at the student's expense, i.e., the students do not get exposure to terminally qualified faculty in most of the junior/senior level courses unless graduate faculty are used for these courses. There is some evidence that the prospective students recognize this "lack of exposure" and may be one reason the department is not recruiting as many high potential students as it could.

Timeline

The following timeline represents my judgments as to the order of specific events needed to implement the strategic plan outlined in this report:

1. Hire Chair, Department of Business, by July 1, 1997.
2. Hire one terminally qualified faculty by July 1, 1997.
3. Implement new organization structure by Fall 1997.
4. Establish new curriculum by Fall 1997. Provide new/existing students with options to switch from old to new courses' requirements.
5. Establish Business Advisory Board by January 1, 1998.
6. Establish internship/mentoring program by Spring 1998.
7. Recruit two new terminally qualified faculty by May 1, 1998 and additional faculty as budget/program growth permits.
8. Be operating under AACSB standards by Fall 1999.

9. Have AACSB consulting team visit in Spring 2000 for preliminary evaluation.
10. Make any program adjustments needed by Fall 2000.
11. Make school year Fall 2000-Spring 2001 the year of record for the AACSB accreditation.
12. Have AACSB accrediting team visit Fall 2002.
13. Receive AACSB accreditation by Spring 2003.

Refer to Exhibit C.2. Based on the assumptions identified in the exhibit's footnotes, the Department of Business could begin making a contribution to total College expenses by the end of the 1999 school year. If the endowment for the Department were slower to materialize than projected, then the ability of the Department to break even and then make a positive contribution to the College budget would be directly affected and would move this critical event further into the future.

Exhibit C.2. Pro Forma Financial Analysis

Year	97-98	98-99	99-00	00-01	01-02
Credit Hours[1]	17,708	18,239	18,786	19,350	19,930
Tuition/CH[2]	$175	190	190	205	205
Revenues	$3,098,900	$3,465,410	$3,569,340	$3,966,750	$4,085,650
Expenses:					
Salaries[3]	$618,516	$805,368	$1,010,904	$1,206,668	$1,331,669
Expenses (Other)[4]	35,667	39,234	43,158	47,473	52,220
Equipment[5]	25,000				25,000
Allocation[6]	2,750,661	2,782,426	2,850,646	2,850,646	2,871,896
Total Expenses	$3,404,844	$3,652,028	$4,129,787	$4,129,787	$4,255,785
Book Profit (Loss)	($305,944)	($186,618)	($302,089)	($163,037)	($170,135)
Endowment Interest[7]	$100,000	$250,000	$500,000	$500,000	$500,000
Contribution	($205,944)	$63,382	$197,911	$366,963	$329,865

[1]Assumes increase of 3 percent in credit hours generated each year.

[2]Assumes tuition increases of $15 per credit hour over current level.

[3]Assumes 10 percent increase in salaries for three years to get to median AACSB levels, thereafter 7 percent per year for merit pay raises plus additional salary for Chairholder and one new faculty and assumes two new terminally qualified faculty per year added at $125,000 for both beginning year 1997-98. The 10 percent increases are to adjust salaries of faculty that are significantly below median levels and are not across-the-board raises.

[4]Assumes 10 percent increase per year.

[5]Assumes 10 Personal Computers purchased @ $2500 each in years 2 and 4.

[6]Assumes allocation increase of 17 percent of increase in salaries.

[7]Assumes total endowment of $5-6 million by 1999-2000.

Appendix D

Strategic Planning Worksheets

PLANNING PROCESS WORKSHEET

This worksheet is provided to aid your institution in starting the strategic planning process. Use the answers to these questions to provide a foundation for completing the remaining worksheets.

1. Who should be involved in the planning process?

    _____

    _____

    _____

2. Who should provide leadership for the strategic planning meetings?

Outside facilitator/consultant	Administrative leader
In-house facilitator	President
Faculty leader	Other:_____

3. Who will ultimately be responsible for arranging sessions and getting material typed, reproduced, and distributed?

    _____

    _____

    _____

4. Who should be responsible for writing and distributing the report documenting the historical trends/current status of the institution?

    _____

    _____

    _____

5. Who will record action taken and how will this information be disseminated?

    _____

    _____

    _____

6. When (at what stage in the process) and how will the staff, board, membership, or others be involved?

    _____

    _____

    _____

7. Where will planning sessions be held?

    _____

    _____

    _____

8. When will planning sessions be held?

    _____

    _____

    _____

9. What is the timetable for completion of the process?

    _____

    _____

    _____

10. What types of background material do participants need prior to starting the first session?

_____

_____

_____

11. What is the scope of this strategic plan (total institution or department, division, program, etc.)?

_____

_____

_____

12. The time horizon of this strategic plan should be:

    1 to 3 years   5 to 10 years
    3 to 5 years   More than 10 years

13. How will the plan be shared with the larger constituency? What approvals are needed? What protocol needs to be observed?

_____

_____

_____

14. Who will train/supervise staff members in working with their own staff and volunteers in setting objectives, developing action plans, and conducting performance appraisals?

_____

_____

_____

15. How frequently will the process be reviewed and by whom?

_____

_____

_____

16. When should this report, which will include input from all the institution's stakeholders and include planning assumptions, Key Result Areas, and the action plan, be approved and distributed?

_____

_____

_____

II. MISSION STATEMENT WORKSHEET

This worksheet will aid you in writing a mission statement for your institution.

1. Write a statement for the following areas:

    Internal operations statement:

    _____

    _____

    _____

    External clientele (environment) statement:

    _____

    _____

    _____

    Describe the internal culture of the institution:

    _____

    _____

    _____

    What needs are served by the institution?

    _____

    _____

    _____

2. Without attempting to write a vision statement at this point, record here some of the items that might appear in a vision statement (see discussion in Chapter 3 for the difference between a vision statement and a mission statement).

    _____

    _____

    _____

3. Now prepare a first draft mission statement:

    _____

    _____

    _____

4. Now evaluate the statement:

    a. Does it define boundaries within which your institution will
       operate?

       _____

       _____

       _____

    b. Does it define the need(s) that your institution is attempting
       to meet?

       _____

       _____

       _____

    c. Does the institution have a local, regional, national, or
       international scope?

       _____

       _____

       _____

    d. Does it define the market (students) that your institution is
       reaching?

       _____

       _____

       _____

   e. Does it include the word "service," or a word with similar meaning?

_____

_____

_____

5. Has there been input from appropriate institutional members?

_____

_____

_____

6. Next, submit it to others familiar with the institution to evaluate your mission statement and offer suggestions on improving the statement. In order words, does the statement say to others what you want it to say?

_____

_____

_____

III. SITUATION ANALYSIS
AND ASSUMPTIONS WORKSHEET

This worksheet will aid you in completing a Strengths, Weaknesses, Opportunities, and Threats (SWOT) analysis.

I. **Step 1. External Environment Analysis:** From community, industry, or institutional surveys and your own sources of information, take your institution's pulse. You are looking for trends—what is going on now and how this relates to past trends that have influenced your institution's performance. From this analysis, list key opportunities and threats for each of the following environmental sectors:

A. Government

Opportunities

1.

2.

3.

Threats

1.

2.

3.

B. Economy

Opportunities

1.

2.

3.

Threats

1.

2.

3.

C. Technology

Opportunities

1.

2.

3.

Threats

1.

2.

3.

D. Social Trends

Opportunities

1.

2.

3.

Threats

1.

2.

3.

E. Students

Opportunities

1.

2.

3.

Threats

1.

2.

3.

F. Funding Sources/Sponsorship

    Opportunities

    1.

    2.

    3.

    Threats

    1.

    2.

    3.

G. Competing Educational Institutions

    Opportunities

    1.

    2.

    3.

    Threats

    1.

    2.

    3.

Next, **evaluate your external analysis:**

- Have you listed several international/national trends that affect your institution?

_____

_____

_____

- Have you listed several local trends that affect your institution?

_____

_____

_____

• Have you identified trends unique to your institution?

_____

_____

_____

• Have you listed several of your most important competitors? What is distinctive about them?

_____

_____

_____

• Which competitors are growing, becoming stronger?

_____

_____

_____

• Which competitors are declining?

_____

_____

_____

• What are the successful ones doing to cause their growth/vibrancy?

_____

_____

_____

II. **Step 2. Internal Operations Analysis:** Using the question guides below and your own information, list key strengths and weaknesses for each of the following sectors of your institution's operations:

A. Management and Planning Systems

   1. Use these questions to help you prepare your strengths and weaknesses list for the management and planning systems portion of your institution's operation:

- Do you have a strategic planning system?

_____

_____

_____

- How does it work?

_____

_____

_____

- Is the institutional structure of your institution allowing effective use of resources?

_____

_____

_____

- Is control centralized or decentralized?

_____

_____

_____

- Are performance measures and information system controls in evidence? What are they?

_____

_____

_____

- What staffing needs do you have?

_____

_____

_____

- Is there a motivation problem? Is it centered in one segment of the institution or is it broadly felt?

  _____

  _____

  _____

- Is your current strategy defined? Is it based upon a strategic plan? Is it working?

  _____

  _____

  _____

- How efficient are operations? Where could improvements be made?

  _____

  _____

  _____

- What is your synopsis of the current management situation? How strong is the management team? Are there obvious weaknesses?

  _____

  _____

  _____

2. Now list the strengths and weaknesses of your management and planning systems:

   - Strengths

     _____

     _____

     _____

- Weaknesses

B. Financial Resources

   1. Use these questions to help you prepare your strengths and weaknesses list for the financial portion of your institution's operation:

- Describe the current financial situation of the institution (number of years operating in the black, current year status, debt load relative to assets and ability to retire debt, whether debt is declining or increasing, any financial statements of the institution, comments of accrediting institutions).

- Do you have regular financial statements prepared? (How complete are they, are they accurate, are they ready by the 15th of the month following, are they distributed on timely bases to everyone having approval authority for an account?)

- What tools would be beneficial in the analysis? (year to date, comparison to a year ago, trends, debt analysis, income analysis, expenditure analysis, comparison to budget)?

   _____

   _____

   _____

- Do you have pro forma statements (see Appendix C) for revenue centers, such as each department/school, etc.?

   _____

   _____

   _____

2. Now list the strengths and weaknesses of your financial resources:

   - Strengths

   _____

   _____

   _____

   - Weaknesses

   _____

   _____

   _____

C. Marketing Resources

   1. Use these questions to help you prepare your strengths and weaknesses list for the marketing portion of your institution's operation:

• Does the institution have established written marketing policies?

_____

_____

_____

• Have you established a written marketing plan outlining what you will and will not do?

_____

_____

_____

• Have you identified your potential students in the written marketing plan?

_____

_____

_____

• Have you identified your funding sponsors (beyond tuition)?

_____

_____

_____

• What are your competitors' services and products, level of demand, and relative market positions?

_____

_____

_____

- What is the structure of tuition and fees charged? How competitive is it?

  _____

  _____

  _____

- What promotional activities (advertising, recruitment strategy) is the institution using? Are there written goals? Is there an advertising budget?

  _____

  _____

  _____

- What is your synopsis of the current marketing situation? How well does the marketing compare to the competition?

  _____

  _____

  _____

2. Now list the strengths and weaknesses of your marketing resources:

   - Strengths

     _____

     _____

     _____

   - Weaknesses

     _____

     _____

     _____

D. Operations or Services Resources

    1. Use these questions to help you prepare your strengths and weaknesses list for the operations or services portion of your institution:

        • What are your operations capacities? (How many students can enroll in your facilities, how many students can be housed and fed, what is an acceptable rate of use?)

        • What is the age and condition of your facilities?

        • What is the age and serviceability of existing equipment (including computers)?

        • What quality control systems are in place?

2. Now list the strengths and weaknesses of your operations or services resources:

• Strengths

_____

_____

_____

• Weaknesses

_____

_____

_____

Next, **evaluate your internal analysis:**

• How many students are you currently serving? (How does this compare to a year ago, a term ago, three years ago?)

_____

_____

_____

III. **Step 3: Development of Assumptions:** List the major assumptions on which the strategic plan is based.

1. _____

_____

2. _____

_____

3. _____

_____

4. _____

_____

5. _____

_____

IV. OBJECTIVES WORKSHEET

This worksheet will aid in developing and testing objectives for a private higher education institution.

I. Developing Objectives

   A. Answer these questions first:

   1. What do the institution's objectives need to relate to—students, faculty/staff, academic programs, funding, or all four? What about other Key Result Areas?

   - _____
   _____

   - _____
   _____

   - _____
   _____

   - _____
   _____

   2. What needs to happen for the institution's programs to be successful? In other words, how many people need to enroll, graduate, publish, obtain grants, contribute, obtain employment, etc.? When do you want these things to happen (give specific date)?

   - _____
   _____

   - _____
   _____

   - _____
   _____

• _____

_____

B. Now write your objectives. Use the information in your answers above to write statements of your objectives for each Key Result Area.

1. Key Result Area No. 1:_____

Objective 1:_____

_____

_____

Objective 2:_____

_____

_____

Objective 3:_____

_____

_____

(Duplicate for each Key Result Area.)

II. Testing Objectives

A. Now test each statement made above using the following criteria:

Is each statement relevant to the basic purpose of your institution?

1._____

2._____

3._____

Is each statement practical?

1._____

2._____

3._____

Does each statement provide a challenge?

1._____

2._____

3._____

Is each stated in objectively measurable terms?

1._____

2._____

3._____

Do you have a specific date for completion?

1._____

2._____

3._____

Does each statement contribute to a balance of activities in line with your institution's strengths and weaknesses?

1._____

2._____

3._____

B. Now test the goal-setting process in the institution:

1. Is there a clear process of setting goals and objectives?

_____

_____

_____

2. What are the goals and objectives for your institution for the current planning year?

_____

_____

_____

3. Is there clear evidence that goals and objectives are written at the institutional level and at the school/college/department level?

_____

_____

_____

4. Do institution-wide level goals and objectives have a clear relationship to vision/mission/purpose?

_____

_____

_____

V. STRATEGY DEVELOPMENT WORKSHEET

This worksheet is provided to help you develop a strategy for your educational institution.

Answer these questions first:

1. What are the distinctive competencies of your institution? What do you do well that makes you different from other higher education institutions?

    _____

    _____

    _____

2. What market segment or segments should you select to match your institution's skills and resources and constituents' needs in those segments?

    _____

    _____

    _____

3. Do you have the skills/resources to pursue several segments or should you concentrate on one segment? Are the financial sponsorship and funding opportunities of that segment large enough to sustain your institution and allow for growth?

    _____

    _____

    _____

Now, develop your positioning statement:

1. Distinctive Competencies

    _____

    _____

    _____

2. Client Segments Sought

_____

_____

_____

3. Services Offered

_____

_____

_____

4. Promotion Orientation

_____

_____

_____

5. Financial Support Levels

_____

_____

_____

6. Growth Orientation

_____

_____

_____

**Next, develop your overall strategy (Growth, Stability, Retrench-
ment) for each major program:**

Major Program_____

<u>Growth (add or expand spectrum of programs)</u>

    Growth: alternative strategy 1
Pros	Cons
1.	1.
2.	2.
3.	3.

    Growth: alternative strategy 2
Pros	Cons
1.	1.
2.	2.
3.	3.

<u>Stability (keep same programs while improving on effectiveness
and efficiency)</u>

    Stability: alternative strategy 1
Pros	Cons
1.	1.
2.	2.
3.	3.

    Stability: alternative strategy 2
Pros	Cons
1.	1.
2.	2.
3.	3.

Retrenchment (major reduction or elimination in existing programs)

Retrenchment: alternative strategy 1

Pros	Cons
1.	1.
2.	2.
3.	3.

Retrenchment: alternative strategy 2

Pros	Cons
1.	1.
2.	2.
3.	3.

Recommended overall strategy for each program

Program:_____

Justification: explain why this is the best alternative.

Pros	Cons
1.	1.
2.	2.
3.	3.

Finally, establish operational strategies for objectives in each Key Result Area in each major program that supports your overall strategy for that program.

An action plan for each Key Result Area should be developed. The action plan places Key Result Areas, objectives, strategies, and action plans into perspective with each other and helps you develop the interrelationships among plans at each institutional level. It helps goals come to life with appropriate action.

ACTION PLAN

OBJECTIVE:_____

_____

STRATEGIES:

     A. _____

           _____

     B. _____

           _____

     C. _____

           _____

     D. _____

           _____

     E. _____

           _____

ACTION PLAN:_____

_____

_____

_____

Person
Responsible:_____

Resources
Required:_____

Date
Started:_____

Date
Completed:_____

VI. EVALUATION AND CONTROL WORKSHEET

This worksheet will aid you in developing tools to measure progress toward your institution's Key Result Area objectives.

Answer the following questions:

1. What kinds of information do you need to evaluate a program's or service's success?

   _____

   _____

   _____

2. Who should receive and review this information?

   _____

   _____

   _____

3. What time periods do you want to use to analyze the data? Weekly? Monthly?

   _____

   _____

   _____

4. What record-keeping system do you need to devise to make sure the information you want is recorded for the time periods you specified in question 3?

   _____

   _____

   _____

Now set up your control procedures:

1. Specify the areas to be controlled:

   A._____

   B._____

   C._____

   D._____

2. Specify the format of the data for each area. (Is it to be numbers by month by program? Do you want number and percentage variations?)

   A._____

   B._____

   C._____

   D._____

3. Specify how the data are to be collected, who is to collect and analyze the data, and who is to receive the results of the analysis:

   A. How will the data be collected?

   _____

   _____

   _____

   B. Who has responsibility to collect and analyze the data?

   _____

   _____

   _____

C. Who is to receive which type of analysis?

   Office   Type of Analysis

_____   _____

_____   _____

_____   _____

_____   _____

4. How will the evaluation take place once the analysis of data has been completed?

_____

_____

_____

Bibliography

Albrecht, K. 1994. *The Northbound Train: Finding the Purpose, Setting the Direction, Shaping the Destiny of Your Organization*. New York: AMACOM.

Barner, R. 1994. *Crossing the Minefield: Tactics for Overcoming Today's Toughest Management Challenges*. New York: AMACOM.

Cope, R., and G. Delaney. 1991. "Academic Program Review: A Market Strategy Perspective." *Journal of Marketing for Higher Education* 3(2) pp. 63-87.

Cope, R.G. 1987. "Opportunity from Strength: Strategic Planning Clarified with Case Examples." *ASHE-ERIC Higher Education Report No. 8*. Washington, DC: Association for the Study of Higher Education.

Cowen, S. 1995. Unpublished presentation at the Council for Adult and Experential Learning Convention, Chicago, IL.

Crispell, D. 1993. *The Insider's Guide to Demographic Know-How*. Burr Ridge, IL: Probus Publishing Company.

Drucker, P. 1954. *The Practice of Management*. New York: Harper.

Drucker, P. 1974. *Management: Tasks, Responsibilities, and Practice*. New York: Harper & Row.

Drucker, P.F. 1989. "What Business Can Learn from Non-Profits." *Harvard Business Review* 67(4) (July-August), pp. 88-93.

Drucker, P.F. 1995. *Managing in a Time of Great Change*. New York: Truman Talley Books/Dutton.

Finzel, H. 1994. *The Top Ten Mistakes Leaders Make*. Wheaton: Victor Books.

Hammer, M., and S.A. Stanton. 1995. *The Reengineering Revolution: A Handbook*. New York: HarperBusiness.

Harvey, P., and J. Sander. 1987. "Charities Need a Bottom Line, Too." *Harvard Business Review* 65 (January-February), pp. 14-22.

High school graduates: Projections by state, 1992 to 2009. (1993). (WICHE Pub. No. 2A239). Boulder, CO: Western Interstate Commission for Higher Education.

Johnston, J. 1996. *Christian Excellence*, 2nd edition. Franklin, TN: JKO Publishing, Inc.

Kaufman, R., and J. Herman. 1991. *Strategic Planning in Education*. Lancaster, PA: Technomic Publishing Co., Inc.

Keller, G. 1983. Shaping an academic strategy. In Keller, G. and Cyert, R. (Eds.) *Academic Strategy*. Baltimore: The Johns Hopkins University Press.

Keller, G. 1993. "Strategic Planning and Management in a Competitive Environment." *New Directions for Institutional Research No. 77*, pp. 9-16.

Keller, G. 1993. "The Changing Milieu for Education Planning." *Planning for Higher Education* 23, pp. 23-26.

Kilmann, R., M. Saxton, R. Serpa, and Associates. 1985. *Gaining Control of the Corporate Culture.* San Francisco: Jossey-Bass.

Kolb, D. 1985. *Learning Style Inventory.* Boston: Mcber and Company.

Kotler, P., and A. R. Andreasen. 1987. *Strategic Marketing for Nonprofit Organizations.* Englewood Cliffs, NJ: Prentice-Hall, Inc.

Kotler, P., and P. Murphy. 1981. "Strategic Planning for Higher Education." *Journal of Higher Education,* 52, 5, pp. 470-489.

Kushel, G. 1991. *Effective Thinking for Uncommon Success.* New York: AMACOM.

McKinnon, N.C. 1994. "Strategic Planning in a Small, Liberal Arts University." *ERIC Descriptive Reports.* Washington, DC: U.S. Department of Education.

Meyer, A. 1991. "What is strategy's distinctive competence?" *Journal of Management,* 17, pp. 821-833.

Mintzberg, H. 1994. *The Rise and Fall of Strategic Planning.* New York: Free Press.

Muczyk, J.P., and B.C. Reimann. 1989. "MBO as a Complement to Effective Leadership." *The Academy of Management Executive,* 3(2), pp. 131-138.

Nadler, D., R. Shaw, A.E. Walton, and Associates. 1994. *Discontinuous Change: Leading Organizational Transformation.* San Francisco: Jossey Bass.

Oosting, K.W. 1968. "Dimensions of Preferred Faculty Environment in Public Junior Colleges." University of Michigan, Ann Arbor: Unpublished doctoral dissertation.

Oosting, K.W. 1996. *Ten Best Managed Christian Liberal Arts Colleges.* Franklin, TN: JKO Publishing, Inc.

Oosting, K.W. and R.B. Allen. 1985. *The College Culture Inventory.* Unpublished manuscript.

Personal & Professional Concerns: Mercy College pegs salaries to enrollment. 1995, July 17. *The Chronicle of Higher Education,* p. A19.

Porter, E. 1989. *Strength Development Inventory.* Pacific Palisades, CA: Personal Strengths Publishing, Inc.

Porter, M. 1980. *Competitive Advantage.* New York: Free Press.

Rivera, D. 1995, June 16. New student group to fight financial-aid cuts. *The Chronicle of Higher Education,* p. A28.

Robinson, C. 1990. "A Study of the Financial Statement Ratios of ECFA Members: An Executive Overview." University of San Francisco: Paper Presentation.

Saffold, G.S. 1994. *Strategic Planning for Christian Organizations: Turning the Power of Vision Into Effective Ministry.* Fayettteville, AR: Accrediting Association of Bible Colleges.

Schein, E. 1985. *Organizational Culture and Leadership.* San Francisco: Jossey-Bass Publishers.

Schneider, B. (ed.). 1990. *Organizational Climate and Culture.* San Francisco: Jossey-Bass.

Shirts, R.G. 1969. *Star Power.* Del Mar, CA: Simile II.

Snyder, H. 1995. *Earth Currents.* Nashville: Abingdon.

Stevens, R., D. Loudon, and W. Warren 1991. *Marketing Planning Guide.* Binghamton, NY: The Haworth Press.

Thomas, K. and R. Kilmann 1974. *The Thomas-Kilmann Conflict Mode Instrument*. Tuxedo, NY: Xicom, Inc.

Thompson, A. Jr., and A.J. Strickland. 1986. *Strategy Formulation and Implementation*. 3rd edition. Plano, TX: Business Publication, Inc.

Wallingford, H., and K. Berger. 1993. "Marketing Strategies for a Low Endowment Private University in the 1990's." *Journal of Marketing for Higher Education* 4(1/2), pp. 325-339.

Index

Page numbers followed by the letter "e" indicate an exhibit.

STRATEGICPLANNING FOR PRIVATE HIGHER EDUCATION

Groups to be served, 65

Haire, Mason, 183
Hamermesh, Richard G., 149
Harvard Psychological Clinic, 73
Herman, J., 89
Hesselbein, Frances, 119
Higher education. *See* Private higher
    education
History, 55
Hood College (Frederick,
    Maryland), 62-63
Hope, managing by, 125
Horizontal axis, 158
Horizontal integration, 155
Human resources, 43

Ideal institutional culture, 78-79
Implementation of differentiation/
    focus strategies, 168-169
Implementation problems, 20-21
Implementation of strategic plan, 45
Importance of planning, 4-5
Improving effectiveness, 169
Income tax structure, changes in, 88
Informal planning, 1
Information flaws, timing of, 186
Informing, 171-172
Innovative, 122
Institution
    appraising, 185
    areas of need, 25-26
    congruent goals of, 138e
    culture within, 77-78
        planning, 82
    determining competency of, 57
    format for strategic planning, 29
    questions to help focus attention,
        33
    reason for being, 66
    reasons for having a mission
        statement, 55
    strategic planning as, *x-xi*

Institution *(continued)*
    types of (Carnegie Commission),
        10-11
Institutional culture
    ideal, 78-79
    measuring, 75-77
    planning, 78
    profile, 97-98
Institutional goals/objectives,
    examples of, 135e
Integration, planning/control,
    184-186
Integrative strategies, 155
Interests, 163
Internal analysis, 93-95
    worksheet, 109-117
Internal culture, 56,71-72
Internal operations and functions, 59
Internal strengths (potential), 101
Internal weakness (potential), 102
Intervening source, consequence
    of, 23
Irrelevance of planning, 19-20

Johnson Bible College (Knoxville,
    Tennessee), 73

Kaufman, R., 89
Keller, George, 85,149
Kellogg Foundation, 19
Key Result Areas, 14,120. *See
    also* Strategic planning
    and academic affairs, 187,188
    and accomplishing objectives,
        25,174
    and action plans, 170
    developing, 19
        ignoring, 18
    establishing, 39-40
    and evaluation/control, 183
    and institutional need, 26
    mission statement as foundation
        for, 54
    and performance, 44,173

Order Your Own Copy of
This Important Book for Your Personal Library!

STRATEGIC PLANNING FOR PRIVATE HIGHER EDUCATION

_____ in hardbound at $49.95 (ISBN: 0-7890-0098-9)

_____ in softbound at $24.95 (ISBN: 0-7890-0191-8)

COST OF BOOKS_____

OUTSIDE USA/CANADA/
MEXICO: ADD 20%_____

POSTAGE & HANDLING_____
(US: $3.00 for first book & $1.25
for each additional book)
Outside US: $4.75 for first book
& $1.75 for each additional book)

SUBTOTAL_____

IN CANADA: ADD 7% GST_____

STATE TAX_____
(NY, OH & MN residents, please
add appropriate local sales tax)

FINAL TOTAL_____
(If paying in Canadian funds,
convert using the current
exchange rate. UNESCO
coupons welcome.)

☐ **BILL ME LATER:** ($5 service charge will be added)
(Bill-me option is good on US/Canada/Mexico orders only;
not good to jobbers, wholesalers, or subscription agencies.)

☐ Check here if billing address is different from
shipping address and attach purchase order and
billing address information.

Signature_____

☐ **PAYMENT ENCLOSED: $**_____

☐ **PLEASE CHARGE TO MY CREDIT CARD.**

☐ Visa   ☐ MasterCard   ☐ AmEx   ☐ Discover

Account # _____

Exp. Date _____

Signature _____

Prices in US dollars and subject to change without notice.

NAME _____

INSTITUTION _____

ADDRESS _____

CITY _____

STATE/ZIP _____

COUNTRY _____ COUNTY (NY residents only) _____

TEL _____ FAX _____

E-MAIL_____
May we use your e-mail address for confirmations and other types of information? ☐ Yes   ☐ No

Order from Your Local Bookstore or Directly from
The Haworth Press, Inc.
10 Alice Street, Binghamton, New York 13904-1580 • USA
TELEPHONE: 1-800-HAWORTH (1-800-429-6784) / Outside US/Canada: (607) 722-5857
FAX: 1-800-895-0582 / Outside US/Canada: (607) 772-6362
E-mail: getinfo@haworth.com
PLEASE PHOTOCOPY THIS FORM FOR YOUR PERSONAL USE.

BOF96